LIGHT FROM
lucas

Lessons in
FAITH
*from a
fragile*
LIFE

BOB VANDER PLAATS
<small>FOREWORD BY</small> Joni Eareckson Tada

"Jesus, who sinned...?"
Jesus answered, "No one sinned.
This came about so that God's works might
be displayed in him."

JOHN 9:1-3

Contents

Foreword

I've gotten used to being on display. Whether it's the child studying my wheelchair, the senior citizen across the way smiling sympathetically, or the waiter eyeing me carefully as I use my bent spoon to eat pieces of hamburger: I'm aware that people are watching. Some might watch out of pity, some out of admiration. All watch, I sense, with unspoken questions. It's part of the territory that comes with living in a wheelchair.

It's what Lucas and his family face every day. But like the Vander Plaats family, I choose to think that people's unspoken questions are, for the most part, good-natured. That's because the author of *Light From Lucas* and I, as followers of Jesus, are constrained to think the best of others. We are called to be on display (as any Christian is). We are encouraged by God's Word to smile from the inside out as the strength of God shows up bountifully through our special challenges. When people eye Lucas in his wheelchair—when people see the smiles on the faces of Bob, Darla, and their sons, I believe they are thinking: *What an amazing family. How great their God must be to inspire such faith and confidence.*

I'm convinced this is why they chose to tell their story in this special book. I don't think they mind the fact that their family is "on display." It's why the book is called *Light From Lucas*. This young man inspired people who observed him. His entire life—with all its challenges and struggles—showcases 1 Corinthians 12:24-26, where we learn "God has combined the members of the body and has given greater honor to the parts that lacked it, so that there should be no division in the body, but that its parts should have equal concern for each other. If one part suffers, every part suffers with it; if one part is honored, every part rejoices with it."

And I can't help but get a lump in my throat when I think that Lucas's dad decided his son's story was important enough to share—share with people like you and me.

No doubt about it. Your thinking will be illumined by the "light" shared in *Light For Lucas*. You will learn about a family whose hearts are settled and whose peace is profound. Don't worry, though—it's not sugarcoated; there are plenty of hard places with which you'll identify. The most important thing you may end up deciding is that if Lucas, by the grace of God, can make it and overcome his limitation, you can to.

Joni Eareckson Tada
Joni and Friends International Disability Center

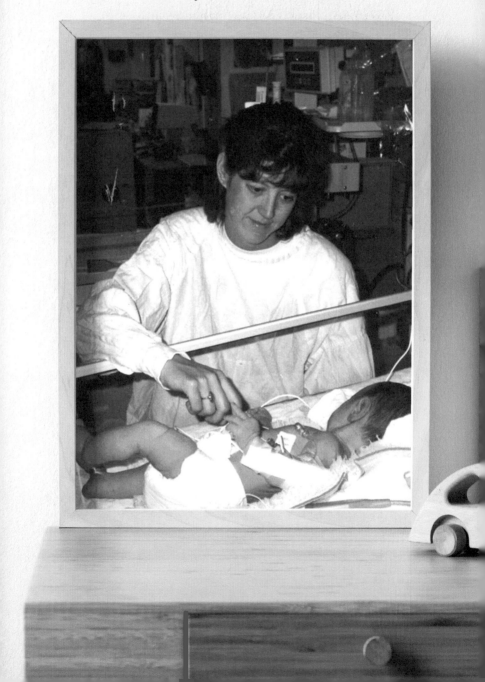

Lucas in the Neo natal Intensive Care Unit
a few days after his birth June, 1993

Expect the Unexpected

"Bob...Bob, wake up! We're going to have our baby." Darla's voice was filled with anticipation and excitement as she informed me that it was time. This Sunday morning would be the day that we would experience the birth of our third child.

We had run this drill twice before; giving birth to two healthy, "normal" boys. Hans was five going on an intellectual fifteen, while Joshua was in the midst of his terrible twos. We felt fully prepared for this baby. Naturally, the baby would have unique personality traits and physical characteristics, but we knew all about the labor and delivery process and the many demands of having a newborn. Although we didn't know the gender of the baby, all of our expectations seemed to be in order.

When I was a high school business teacher and basketball coach I would tell my students of my ambition to have five sons. I would joke with them about my plans to create the perfect basketball team, composed solely of my own genetics.

I had already identified Hans as my point guard. He was gifted at handling the ball and had an uncanny feel for the game. Joshua would be my shooting guard. He loved shooting. He also loved kicking, hitting, and anything else that would produce offensive assault on a worthy opponent. Uncles Stan and Jerry were his favorite targets.

This Sunday, June 13, 1993, I was certain that Darla would deliver another member of the perfect starting line-up.

Maybe he would be a talented forward; the perfect compliment to the skill sets of Hans and Josh. I was well on my way to coaching a championship team composed exclusively of my own genetics. Wow!

Unfortunately, the plans I teased my students about were quickly thwarted when reality proved much differently than lighthearted anecdotes. Darla did indeed give birth to a son, but thoughts of championship basketball games grew faint as our delivery room drama unfolded.

The baby was breached in the birth canal, preventing a vaginal delivery. I looked on as the doctors and nurses administered Darla with an epidural and began cutting into her. I looked on as our son was brought harshly into the world, and I looked on as the medical personnel rushed around him with urgency signaling that something was very wrong.

His head was abnormally large and completely out of proportion with his frail body. His lips and skin were parched blue, craving oxygen. He wasn't pinking-up which heightened the suspicions of everyone in the room. As I looked on in fear, the doctor took me by the arm and led me away from the commotion. He had ordered an air ambulance to transport our newborn son from our hometown hospital in Sheldon, Iowa, to a better equipped hospital in Sioux City. The words that he spoke still ring in my head today, "Babies with issues don't belong in rural hospitals."

Issues? What does he mean, "Babies with issues?"
This is my baby...Darla's baby...a future member of
the Vander Plaats basketball team Darla and I were

the perfect couple...we started out in the church nursery together...we were classmates and high school sweethearts...we have two normal sons and now we have a baby with issues? It didn't make any sense to me. Thoughts whirled through my mind relentlessly, yet I was determined to remain calm on the outside; appearing strong for Darla and those attending our son.

In the midst of this sudden sea of instability, I reached for stability by phoning our parents. This birth announcment was quite unlike those we made with Hans and Josh. It was void of laughter, excitement, and statistical information. Instead it was one of stunned reality and requests for help. "Mom, can you stay with Darla at the Sheldon Hospital? Dad, can you go with me to St. Luke's in Sioux City? Can you make the necessary phone calls to family and friends? Dan and Beth, can you look after Hans and Josh? *Please* tell everyone to pray for the son we've yet to hold."

Circumstances were spinning out of control and I was pretending to be strong. Friends, doctors, family members, nurses, strangers, flight technicians, and people requesting signatures came in and out of my confused consciousness, yet I can recall them with vivid detail.

Kissing Darla goodbye, I headed for the van. My dad was with me as I began the one hour drive to Sioux City, yet words are inadequate to describe the intense loneliness I felt as the helicopter carrying our son passed overhead. I was completely helpless. The drive was consumed with rushing thoughts and questions. *I don't even know him...he is my son and I can't do a thing for him. Will he be alright? What went wrong? How is Darla? What about Hans and Josh? What will the future hold? Where is God? What if our baby dies? What if he lives?*

When we reached the hospital we were quickly directed to the neonatal intensive care area. The specialists explained the best-case scenario first; saying that our son could just be a big baby, with a big head, struggling to breathe. The optimist in me became hopeful. Then they explained numerous other possibilities. He could have a syndrome that would go undiagnosed for several months. He may have birth defects that could result in a multitude of disabilities. His cranium could be filled with fluid and house little to no brain, resulting in death within weeks or even days. My rising hopes were dashed as I signed for the necessary tests.

Once the tests had begun, the rushing stopped. It was time to catch my breath and begin processing the chaos. After a deep sigh and a moment of prayer, I picked up the phone to call Darla. She was surely experiencing the same numb helplessness. A mother is designed to nurse, bond, and care for her newborn. This process had been coldly interrupted with the chopping of helicopter propellers and now she sat in a hospital surrounded by people...all alone. No Bob. No Hans. No Josh. No baby. She was left with bland walls and recovery procedures, enduring physical and emotional pain.

Our phone conversation was mostly business. We discussed the doctor's information in detail. To the best of my ability, I described the tests that were being performed on our son and we talked about the range of possibilities, from mild to severe disabilities...from normal to dead. Words were sober as our phone call drew to a close and the question that Darla asked me still sends a chill down my spine, "What are we going to do if he's not right?" The emotion in her voice characterized our fear. We were adrift by the unraveling of the day, and terrified by the future. What began as excited anticipation and predictability had turned into a moment by moment battle for composure.

I am rarely at a loss for words, but Darla's question hit me like a ton of bricks and I clambered for an answer. What *will* we do if he isn't right? I paused in silence, remembering my role in this reality drama. *I am the man...I am supposed to be tough...I should be able to handle anything that comes my way.* My voice was quiet and broken as I said, "We'll get through it... we'll get through it."

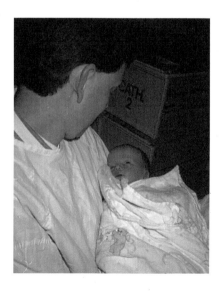

Dear Lucas,

I love you! I wish I could have expressed my love for you on the day you were born, but the doctors and nurses wouldn't let me near you. And, to be honest, I didn't know if I wanted to be close to you at the time.

It still bothers me that your mom and I were not able to appropriately welcome you into the world, and into our love and care. Your traumatic birth surprised everyone...including Mom and me. We were scared for you and scared for us.

During the nine months that your body was being knit together, you were housed, protected, and nourished by your mom. Just like Hans and Josh, you and Mom bonded during pregnancy. It is a beautiful process and one of God's greatest gifts to mothers. Mom loved being pregnant and she was good at it. ☺

You need to know that your mom paid attention to every detail during your incubation. She loves to read and read everything she could find to enhance your development in the womb. But, regardless of the many pages she read, there weren't any books or warning signs to adequately prepare us for your birth.

God made only one YOU...for only one US.

The separation you felt at the time of your birth was a parting from Mom. The separation Mom felt was a parting from you. I didn't feel any immediate separation...I felt confused and disappointed. You were not *what I was looking for and I really didn't know you. You see, dads are spectators in the pregnancy game. Yeah, I enjoyed putting on a good show to convince people that I felt just as pregnant and attached to you as Mom did, but the fact is...I didn't have a clue.*

I had no idea how God would use you and your unique abilities to impact my self-absorbed life.

It is a privilege to dedicate this book to you, Lucas. You have taught me many life lessons and it is my hope that relaying these lessons will impact the lives of many others.

Thanks for accepting me. Thanks for teaching me. Thanks for loving me. And thanks for bringing so much joy to my life.

I love Lucas...I love Lucas. Yes, I do! Yes, I do!
He's my buddy, buddy...buddy, buddy, buddy.
I love you...I love you!

I do love you, Lucas; more today than the day you were born, more tomorrow than today.

Dad

[To the readers: "I Love Lucas" is a song I sing to Lucas, to the tune of "Frère Jacques."]

Make It Count

I was a five-year-old kindergartener, still sleeping in a bed against the back wall of my parents' bedroom. With six kids and one on the way, we were running out of sleeping quarters in our two-story, middle-class home. The bed my oldest brother slept in was curiously positioned in the hallway at the top of the stairs, just above the entryway. Although we were cramped for space, I believe its location had more to do with strategy than necessity; allowing Mmom and Dad to keep a close eye on a teenage son in the prime of sowing his wild oats.

My first vivid memory came early one morning when my dad sat down on my bed to wake me up and deliver some eagerly awaited news, Mom had just given birth to our newest sibling. I remember being instantly excited as I waited for the details. Was it a girl or a boy? What was the baby's name? I was finally a big brother! Instead of giving me the particulars, Dad informed me that I would not be going to school that day. My baby brother had been stillborn…DOA…dead on arrival. The thrill of exciting news was quickly followed by a crushing blow and confused disappointment.

Although the events that followed are less clear to me, I do remember standing at the graveside funeral with my dad and siblings. We were joined by a few friends and relatives, and our pastor. Mom was still in the hospital recuperating from childbirth, so she was unable to attend the service. As I stood quietly next to Dad, my eyes moved back and forth between the little white box holding the baby brother that I had so anxiously awaited and the tiny void in the ground which would soon become his body's home.

From my earliest memory, I have had cause to contemplate death.

A short time later, I noticed a framed photograph in our living room of a beautiful little girl with dark hair and blue eyes. I remember asking Mom who the girl was and why we had a picture of her. After a long pause, Mom replied, "That is your sister, Barbie." Really? I didn't even know that I had a sister named Barbie. She went on to explain how Barbie had a very rare type of kidney disease, and that they had traveled with her frequently to the University of Iowa Hospitals for diagnoses and treatments.

In the winter of Barbie's kindergarten year she became ill with flu-like symptoms. Mom explained how she suspected the symptoms indicated more than a seasonal virus and decided to take Barbie to the doctor on a Monday. After gathering the information concerning her lack of appetite and inability to keep food down, the doctor reasonably concluded that it was merely the flu. Still sensing a bigger issue, they returned to the doctor each day that week only to be sent home time and time again. By Sunday morning, Mom's perseverance won out and Barbie was admitted to the hospital. Sunday afternoon, Christmas Day, Barbie died due to heightened complications of her kidney disease brought on by the flu.

Once again, at a very young age, I had cause to contemplate death.

By the summer of 1979, I had grown into an invincible sixteen-year-old, enjoying the independence of having my own driver's license. One hot July night, after cruising the streets of our small town in my '67 Buick Skylark, I managed to arrive home right at midnight, just in time to meet my Friday night curfew.

Brian, my older brother, was already asleep in the room we shared and had our window propped open, hoping for an occasional cool breeze. I slipped into bed and was just dozing off when I heard a car speed into our driveway. The front door flew open then quickly slammed shut as our oldest and married brother, Stan, ran up the stairs and down the hall to our parents' bedroom. He spoke with great intensity as he told them to wake up and get dressed, and explained that their fourth oldest child Harlan, a.k.a. Hawk, had been severely injured in a car crash. We needed to get to Sioux Falls, South Dakota, as quickly as possible.

The terror still resonates in my mind today when I force myself to remember the details of those early morning moments. I climbed into the family car with my mom and dad, and brother Brian. Stan arranged for Vern, a family friend, to drive the seventy-mile journey for us. It was a quiet ride. My mom was stunned silent, only voicing a few deep sighs and an occasional cry of "why" in prayer.

My dad was the man. Clearly he was concerned about the condition of his son, but he remained remarkably composed; a source of strength for the rest of us. Little did I know that his example would prove to be so precious when I faced the fear of losing my own son years later. Dad asked Vern to give him the details of the situation. How did it happen? Who was involved? How are the others doing?

The answers made us all aware of the seriousness of the accident. Harlan's girlfriend and the other female passenger were taken to a local hospital and both were expected to make full recoveries. Vern went on to explain that Dennis, the driver of the car, was "no longer with us." Dennis and Harlan had both been on the driver's side of the vehicle, which absorbed the fatal blow of the collision. The statement, "He's no longer with us" rendered all other details of the accident insignificant. All we were told about Harlan was that he was found unresponsive at the scene, but still breathing on his own. He was in trouble.

When we finally arrived at the hospital our family gathered in the intensive care waiting area. We didn't know what to think or how to act. The doctor finally arrived to inform us that there was little hope for recovery of any kind. Harlan's brain stem looked as if it had been cut with a knife due to the whiplash force of the impact. He was holding on by a very thin thread.

Harlan hung on by that thread for five days. Our family rode the waves from hope to despair. At times we prayed, "Please allow him to live" and other times we prayed, "Please take him quickly." The waiting area had become our home since the time of the accident, and on the fifth day our entire family was called to be by Harlan's bedside.

The timing of this request seemed ironic, since it came almost immediately after Mom and Dad had returned to the waiting area with renewed hope and optimism. You see, each night they would go together, just the two of them, to say a prayer at Harlan's bedside. Mom would hold his hand as Dad prayed for divine intervention and for God's will to be done. On this night, Harlan squeezed Mom's hand and pulled it over his heart. What we had interpreted as cause for optimism, was actually his way of affirming his love and...saying good-bye.

Nevertheless, when the nurses suggested that the family should gather in his room, we did not question them. We moved quickly to his hospital bed, working our way around monitors and life-support equipment. Our family held hands as my oldest brother offered a prayer. When he ended his prayer with "Amen," the repetitive beeping of the heart monitor became a single tone and the screen revealed a straight line. It was a moment of comfort I will always hold dear, for at that very moment we knew that Harlan had transitioned from his earthly home to his heavenly one.

At the invincible age of sixteen, I again had cause to contemplate death.

The deaths of my three siblings have had a major impact on my life. We cannot know when, where, or how we are going to die. The only certainty is that death *is* certain, the mortality rate is still holding at 100%.

Although the reality of their lives and deaths has given me much to ponder, it is Lucas' that has taught me the incredible frailty of our existence. Right from his first breath he has been teetering on the bridge between life and death; existing in a whirlwind of watchful eyes and medical equipment.

By his fifteenth month, I had been called on twice to revive him, rescue breathing while 911 was called. Both times resulted in emergency helicopter rides, and both times I was reminded of the great importance of counting his days...giving thanks for every moment. It was soon after these experiences that I promised myself to do everything in my power to make his life count, regardless of its certain brevity.

As a result of these episodes, the doctors determined his condition to be seizure related, modified his meds and prescribed food supplements for weight gain. Lucas rallied quickly and became quite healthy despite his odd exterior. His large head, way out of proportion with his frail body, even prompted one of our son's friends to refer to Lucas as "E.T." Although the comment was hurtful, it was an accurate description of his appearance.

By the time he reached fifteen months, he was averaging a life flight every five months. Although this is not a desirable statistic, it was the only thing he had on his brothers, who thought riding in a helicopter would be very cool.

It was this third helicopter emergency that was different in one aspect. After Lucas was stabilized in the intensive care unit and connected to all the proper equipment, the doctors presented us with a question that we had not been asked before, "If Lucas stops breathing or begins deteriorating in condition, do you want us to implement life-saving measures or would you rather we just make him comfortable?" We were taken aback by the reality of his words, but the answer came quickly for both of us...revive him.

Once again, I had cause to contemplate death. Darla and I began discussing it with sobering frequency, specifically Lucas' death.

When I was a high school principal in Sheldon, we lived in a home near the local cemetery. Frequently, after a long day at school, I would go for a walk. It helped me to process the day's events and prepare for upcoming meetings and activities. These walks undoubtedly took me through the beautifully quiet cemetery pathways. The stars seemed brighter there and the colors more vivid.

The sound of my footsteps was most humbling, as I walked and studied the tombstones. I noticed that some told the tale of long and full existence, while others reflected abbreviated life; way too short in my opinion. I would walk along, surveying the name, date of birth, date of death, epitaph, and other unique characteristics written on each tombstone trying to gain a glimpse into each person's life.

My walks usually progressed to the west side of the cemetery, along Union Avenue, where I would stop and reflect on the gravesites of my three siblings. There were Hawk, Barbie, and my baby brother Bradley. As I studied their names, I thought of how great it would be to have them there with me; laughing, talking, knowing one another's spouses and children. Then I would think to myself, "Let me get this straight. They are in heaven and I want them in Sheldon?" My conclusion was always the same. I was being selfish.

One day, after hearing a message by Lou Holtz[1], the famed football coach, I was inspired to view the tombstones of that cemetery in an entirely new way; all exactly alike, with one symbolic difference...the dash. Each one had the same statistical elements, but the dash that was placed between the date of birth and the date of death represented each one's contribution to life. I began to view the dash as a symbol of the impact each person had in their abundance or lack of time on earth. Since that day, my focus has changed from contemplating the number of days, to the impact of days. Whether given one minute or one hundred years, God intends for each of us to make a contribution.

Lucas' days may not be as many, or as normal, as we would like, but I am confident that they have been purposeful. His life has inspired me to seek my own purpose with passion and to motivate others to do the same. Lucas has taught me the importance of living my *dash* to its fullest.

Are you determined to make *your* dash count? Maybe you are thinking, "What could I possibly contribute? I'm not a gifted poet like Shakespeare, a humanitarian like Mother Teresa, or a genius like Einstein. I just get up each day, take care of business, and try to stay out of trouble." True. Maybe some lives are less public and profound than others, but no life is without significance.

Ephesians 2:10 says, "For we are God's workmanship, created in Christ Jesus to do good works, which God prepared in advance for us to do." God has a purpose for every human life. He has planned for you to do things that no one else can do.

The significance doesn't lie in the grandiosity of our

contribution, but in the heart of it. If you are called to be at home with our children, you must do it with passion. If you are called to start your own business, you must do it with passion. If you are called to teach, you must do it with passion. Whatever you are called to do, you must do it with passion! There will always be someone who is more talented or better prepared, but Psalm 139:13-14 says, "For you [God] created my inmost being; you knit me together in my mother's womb. I praise you because I am fearfully and wonderfully made." He designed each of us perfectly, with all we need to accomplish that which He has planned for us.

Some may look at Lucas and wonder what purpose he could possibly fulfill, but he too is *fearfully and wonderfully made* with everything he needs to complete his calling. He cannot walk, or read, or speak. He will never be a doctor, or a lawyer, or a father. He requires full-time care to meet his physical needs. Yet he has a unique and significant purpose that only he can fulfill and his *dash* will have impact.

Contemplating death may be necessary at times, but it is far better to contemplate life! Dream big and search for your significance relentlessly. You didn't choose the day you were born, you cannot know how many days you have before you will die, but you can determine how you will live today.

Make the decision to laugh more often, take more risks, love more deeply, complain less, help a neighbor, offer a kind word, clean up a mess that isn't yours, forgive someone or say *I'm sorry*, say *thank you*, pray for a friend, pray for a stranger, learn something new, set a new goal. Little by little, the choices you make today are writing your story. Whether you're given a few more hours or many more years, choose to make a difference; to live your *dash* with passion and make every moment count.

Dear Lucas,

Your life has taught me so much.

I love to go on cruises with you. It is priceless to see your face as you sit in the copilot's chair anticipating the start of the engine. I get so much joy from watching your excitement as the engine ignites and the music begins to play. I love it when you clap your chest, stiffen your body, and sing in your own beautiful way to the music.

When you once settle into the ride and relax, the squint of your nose, the wrinkles by your eyes, and the coo in your voice tells me that you feel blessed. The little things - yeah, the little things - are what give you joy. Because of you, they give me joy too. Thanks for reminding me of life's simple pleasures!

If it were up to me, I would remove all of your disabilities. You would have no more pain. You would have no more fear. You would walk. You would run. You would play. You would be completely healthy. More than anything, you would talk. You would share your thoughts, your hopes, your fears, and your dreams.

The irony in my wishes is that I would be robbing your life of God's purpose. Your life, your near-death experiences, your pain, your seizures, and your disabilities have had a positive impact on many lives. Because of you, others have been drawn closer to God and have been challenged to discover their purpose.

I'm sure you notice that some people don't really know how to respond to you. Some, verbally and non-verbally, question your existence because you don't look "normal" to them. Our "Victoria Secret" world isn't made for you and, on many levels, you can be really thankful for this.

It may not be easy, but don't worry about those who are unwilling to embrace your uniqueness. Instead, focus on those people who are inspired by it!

Hans writes your name on the inside of his basketball shoes to remind him that any challenge he may face pales in comparison to your daily obstacles. Mom and I have moved and changed careers to maximize the impact our lives, and your life, will have according to God's perfect will.

Your life has motivated others to maximize their impact here on earth. More so, your life encourages others to contemplate the Creator. Don't ever forget that your life has a unique purpose, Lucas.

I thank God for your life and I thank you for living it with passion!

It Could Be Worse

What is my problem? Why am I so sad? Not only do I lack joy, I feel deprived...robbed of luxuries that are found in the lives of others and tired of living with situations that seem so unfair. Sound familiar? In 1995, I found myself asking these questions, feeling angry and discouraged.

For years, Darla and I have had a typical Sunday morning drill. We corral the kids in the car, arriving at church with just enough time to offer a few greetings before taking our seats in our favorite pew. After the service, the boys make their way to their Sunday school classes, while Darla and I go to our class, grabbing a cup of coffee and a pastry on the way.

One such Sunday we were visiting with friends in the hallway after class, waiting for Hans and Josh to rejoin us. Darla was holding Lucas and talking with a group of ladies, while I discussed last night's game with Dave, Bruce, and Denny. All at once Darla motioned to me, her face dressed in fear. Lucas, who was fifteen months, was turning blue...not breathing. I scooped him up and rushed to an empty classroom to begin rescue breathing measures, asking a friend to call 9-1-1.

By the time the ambulance arrived, Lucas was breathing, but his breaths were shallow and labored.

The emergency room was a flurry of activity by the time we arrived, and we could hear the nurse hollering, "It's Lucas!" He had developed quite a reputation in his short time on earth.

The doctors were able to get him stabilized, but wanted

LIGHT FROM LUCAS

to fly him to a hospital in Sioux Falls, South Dakota, for further treatment and observation. Darla accompanied Lucas in the helicopter, while I stayed in Sheldon long enough to get Hans and Josh delivered to family members.

In the quiet hours, driving to Sioux Falls in our van, I was consumed with thoughts of *Why me? Why Lucas? Why our family?* I was focused on myself and indulging in a pity that seemed well-warranted.

Arriving at the hospital, I found my way to the intensive care room. Darla and Lucas were there with the doctor and I was given an assessment of Lucas' condition. As the doctor concluded his update, he asked the question that had become soberly familiar, "If the events of this morning are repeated in this hospital room in Sioux Falls, do you want us to implement life-saving measures to save Lucas?"

Our answer remained the same, "Of course, we want you to revive him." The doctor's question was not a new one, but it struck me with new emotion. It seemed as though he was questioning the *worth* of Lucas' life...was it a life worth saving.

The recent months had drawn me close to mental collapse. We had been through more than a year of uncertainty with Lucas, while still trying to raise our other two sons and maintain a sense of normalcy in our home. Some brand of breakdown seemed to be looming and this latest visit to the ICU produced an insatiable need to catch my breath. I had convinced myself that I was not allowed the privilege of showing emotion. Darla and the boys needed to see a strong husband

and father, able to stay composed and in control.

As I stepped out of Lucas' room, my eyes glimpsed to the room of another little boy and my selfish thoughts were quickly diverted. This preschooler didn't appear to have a physical or mental disability. He didn't appear to have breathing problems or a seizure disorder. In fact, he appeared to be completely normal. This little boy was apparently healthy, but sat in the intensive care unit crying out in pain because someone had used a cigarette as a means to discipline, burning his flesh from the top of his head to the soles of his little feet.

God used that scene to crash my pity party in dramatic fashion, and the message was loud and clear...*it could be so much worse.*

When I was a preschooler, sleeping in a crib in my parents' room, self-preservation was never a concern. My parents always cared for me, always protected me, and always loved me. My home was a place of safety, never one of fear.

Regardless of Lucas' fragile condition, his experience with invasive medical procedures, his inability to participate in normal boyhood activities, and his constant fight for survival, at least we could be certain that he was loved. Darla and I, his brothers, grandparents, extended family, and many family friends surrounded him with love and kindness. His wellbeing had always been a priority.

Still standing in the hospital hallway, my mind drifted to my experiences as a high school principal, witnessing too many teenagers becoming parents - children having children. I contemplated the life of Lucas in the hands of a teenage mother or in the hands of an abusive father. My heart cried out in repentance, *it could be worse.*

I was suddenly filled with gratitude that Lucas did indeed belong to me, to *our* family. God seemed to be saying, "Quit whining and hold your head up. Get things into perspective, and get on with life."

At family gatherings, my older brother, Brian, is often heard saying, "What about me?" He wants us to pay attention to him. Now, if you think that to be odd behavior for a man in his forties, you're right. Nevertheless, it always gets a laugh, gaining him the attention he desires.

Most of us have not made a habit of verbalizing the question, "What about me?" But we ask it repeatedly through our attitudes and actions. We are flooded with vanity every time we turn on the television or look at a magazine. *You owe it to yourself...If it feels good, do it...Have it your way.* Our society puts a priority on self-indulgence, convincing us that we must satisfy our own need for happiness before we will ever be able to please others.

We are a long way from the attitude of President Kennedy when he admonished his fellow Americans to, "Ask not what your country can do for you, ask what you can do for your country."[2] Instead, we have become more about receiving than giving. We have become obsessed with self-gratification and the accumulation of material possessions.

The danger of putting a priority on personal fulfillment is addressed very directly in Luke 12:16-21. Jesus tells the tale of a farmer with a bumper crop. The man's land produces such a large crop that he has no place to store the excess, so he decides to tear down his barns and build bigger barns. Seems logical, doesn't it? He boasts that he has enough food to last many years, ensuring a carefree future. Although it seems logical, even responsible, God calls him a fool and explains that he will die long before he is able to enjoy what he has accumulated.

If Jesus would have ended the tale there, it might leave us to assume that God is against wealth and responsible planning for the future, but that wasn't the end of the story. The last sentence of Chapter 12 reveals the moral, "This is how it will be with anyone who stores up things for himself but is not rich toward God." God is not displeased with possessions, but He is passionate about priorities. When we spend more time and energy making our lives more comfortable here on earth than we spend seeking a relationship with God, we are fools.

God wants us to take the focus off of ourselves and become consumed with Him. He wants us to seek His face before we trace His hand. If the farmer had sought the face of God, rather than finding security in material abundance, he may have realized that there was far more joy and fulfillment to be gained by blessing those around him.

In Luke 12:31-34, after telling the story of the farmer, Jesus says, "But seek His kingdom, and these things will be given to you as well. Do not be afraid, little flock, for your Father has been pleased to give you the kingdom. Sell your possessions and give to the poor. Provide purses for yourselves that will not wear out, a treasure in heaven that will not be exhausted, where no thief comes near and no moth destroys. For where your treasure is, there your heart will be also."

God doesn't promise us wealth, life without struggle, or children born without disabilities. He simply wants us to remember that He has already given us *everything*. When Jesus died and rose again to save us from our sin, He gave us the Kingdom; an eternal treasure that cannot be stolen or destroyed. Jesus' words in the above passage are a gentle reminder that our focus (*for where your treasure is*) will determine our happiness (*there your heart will be also*).

I believe that God was speaking to me that day in the hospital hallway, reminding me to major in the majors and to seek Him first. Lucas will never bring home a bumper sticker that says "My Kid Is on the Honor Roll." We will never hear the crowd cheer for him as he makes a game-winning shot. He will never captivate an audience with musical talent. But when he hears me sing *I love Lucas, I love Lucas* his face shines with a smile that fills my heart with immeasurable joy. That is what I treasure. I must determine to be so swept away with what he *is* able to do, that his deficiencies become secondary.

In the eyes of this world, Lucas' contribution to life could be better. But it could also be worse. Our journey with Lucas has challenged us to continually evaluate our perspective. Throughout this book we talk at length about focus and perspective. You may be thinking, "Okay, I've got it!" But do you? Do you make it through a week, or a day, without worrying or complaining about a difficult circumstance? Are you focused on temporal pleasures or eternal rewards? Do you spend more time blessing others than seeking your own pleasure? Do your attitudes and actions reflect one that fully understands that *it could be worse*?

Parents often ask their children, "How many times do I have to tell you...?" I suppose that our heavenly Father could ask us the same question, yet his patience and grace are unmatched. He wants us to be satisfied and to trust Him completely, yet we fail over and over again. We feel deprived. We get stuck in a state of discouragement. And we question God's plan. Just as parents use consequences to shape the character of their children, God uses the situations of our lives to make us stronger and to remind us that this life is temporary.

It saddens me to think of what God must have thought as he observed my pity party the day I drove to the Sioux Falls Hospital. If He had been there in flesh, I imagine that He may have challenged me, saying, "I love Lucas more than you ever could. He is my son, too. *Please* stop concentrating on your perceived injustice, and simply trust me. Focus on what you do have. You have the opportunity to hold him, to watch him clap his hands, and to laugh with him. Having Lucas is helping you to understand My sufficiency, and to depend on it, because it has made you painfully aware of your own insufficiency. You are learning that grumbling about your situation won't change a thing. Bob, it isn't a perfect life that will make your joy complete, but a perfect God. Someday Lucas will be fully restored, but today he is yours to love...just as he is."

When I ran for governor of the state of Iowa in 2002, I participated in several debates with my fellow candidates.

These situations could be quite intimidating. Several undetermined questions would be asked by panelists, and sometimes opponents. The lights were bright and hot. There were reporters, cameras, and microphones surrounding us. I knew that I must be flawless in order to gain the needed support, and every eye in the room seemed to be staring right at me.

Every time I participated in a debate, I would place a photograph of Lucas on my podium. Following one such event, an opponent inquired about the photo. I explained that seeing the picture of Lucas reminded me that things really aren't that bad. The worst thing that could possibly happen while campaigning wouldn't compare with what Lucas must endure every day. It reminded me that my situation could be worse.

Companies spend millions of dollars convincing us that we need a new car, nicer house, and perfect children in order to be happy. Sadly, we often believe it, but how would our attitudes be different if we reminded ourselves daily that *it could be worse*? When our boys are running and screaming through the house, getting on our nerves, Darla and I thank God that they can speak and that they have legs that work.

Looking at Lucas causes me to ask the question, "What is my problem?" He has taught me to make every day a good day. I can walk and run. I can talk and sing. My body is healthy. Lucas has given me a fresh appreciation for my abilities, and has inspired me to give more of myself, more of my talents, more of my resources, more of my energy. He has taught me that things could be so much worse. He has taught me that true joy is only found when I surrender my desires and frustrations, fully trusting God's sufficiency, and focus diligently on the blessings in my life.

Dear Lucas,

You've been through so much: five helicopter rides, three resuscitations, a few code blues, countless seizures, and one major surgery. You have a tracheotomy to help you breathe and the doctors are still talking about giving you a feeding tube.

For all of your thirteen years on this earth you've been unable to walk, run, read, or talk. In addition to these physical and medical limitations, you live away from home and don't have the opportunity to experience daily life with your family on a regular basis.

According to many people's standards, your life-condition could not be worse. But before you go thinking "Duh" and begin having a pity party, I want you to focus on what you do have.

You live in a great country. Your doctors, nurses, educators, therapists, and caregivers are among the best in the world. You are alive and experiencing a great quality of life because of America's expertise, generosity, and compassion.

You are surrounded and engulfed in love. I love you. Mom loves you. Your brothers love you. Your grand-

pas and grandmas love you. Your uncles and aunts love you, and Ruth loves you. Most importantly, God loves you!

Because of this love, your needs will always be met. And because of this love, you have everything!

Time and time again, I've seen you bring out the best in others. In evaluating life, I don't believe that we will be measured according to what we accomplished for ourselves, but according to what we have done for others. And based on that measurement, you are living a great life!

Lucas, don't ever forget that your life could be worse. You have the best of care, the best of love, and you bring out the best in others. Above all, you have hope. The God who created and loves you will someday welcome you into Heaven with the gift of a perfect body, full of glory and power (1 Corinthians 15:42-44). That will be an awesome day!

As I've told you before, you are not the child I prayed for, but I am so thankful you are the child I received. You have taught me to appreciate the "things" in life that have eternal value, and for that I am eternally grateful.

Keep on being a blessing, Lucas! I love you.

Dad

Don't Wear Masks

Arthur Fonzerelli...Fonzie...the Fonz. He was the great role model and fashion icon of my adolescence. Fonzie was cool.

In the spring of 1977 I was in eighth grade and my track team was participating in a multischool meet at Northwestern College in Orange City, Iowa. Track athletes dressed differently in 1977, than they do today. We didn't wear full warm-ups or carry matching duffle bags. Instead, we boarded the track bus in blue jeans and jean jackets because we were trying to be cool...like Fonzie.

Our team arrived at the college and took its place on the field inside the track where we would wait for our chosen events to be announced. When I heard the call for the high-jump, I removed my jean jacket to expose my Sheldon Christian Meteors jersey, something I was very proud to wear, and began preparing for the event.

As I finished a series of stretches, standing among my teammates, I removed my blue jeans. About that time, there was a roar of laughter. Being distracted, I had missed the joke, but laughed anyway because that's what middleschoolers do: Even if you don't know why they're laughing, when your friends laugh, you laugh. So I was enjoying the moment until Fred said, "Hey, Bob, you forgot your shorts!"

There I stood in my chosen underwear for the day! But just like Fonzie, I stayed cool.

After pulling my jeans back on, I found our coach and explained my dilemma. He quickly spotted Johnny and called him over. Now Johnny was not built like a typical track athlete. Johnny was quite round. Coach told him to give me his shorts, so Johnny and I were off to the locker room.

As soon as I put the shorts on, I knew I had a problem. They were never going to stay on my waist, especially during a high jump competition! "Last call for the high jump," came booming over the loud speaker. I rushed back to my coach, who proceeded to wrap the waistband of my shorts...Johnny's shorts...with athletic tape. I still can't believe that I let him do that! Despite all of the excitement, I made it to the high jump in time to compete and was doing surprisingly well. In fact, I made it to the final group of three and was preparing to attempt a jump which would beat my personal best.

As I prepared, I spotted Rhonda. Rhonda was a high-jumper from another team, and Rhonda was a babe! If I could clear the bar *and* keep my shorts up, I might have a shot with her. It was a true "wonder years" moment.

I concentrated. I visualized a successful jump. Adrenaline rushed through my body as I ran the path and approached the bar. As soon as my feet left the ground I knew I was going to make it. It was the best jump of my life. I cleared the bar by a couple of inches and the tape around my waist stayed intact. Rhonda was as good as mine. Regrettably, I jumped too close to the corner, flew *past* the landing mat and my body slammed onto the asphalt track. I was bloody, with black tar embedded in my backside. But, just like Fonzie, I stayed cool.

Everyone was looking at me, watching me, and talking about my ridiculous landing. My chances with Rhonda were definitely done.

Looking back over the years, I realize that the opinions of others have always mattered a great deal to me; specifically, their opinions about *me*.

One of the traditions our society has established is the insincerity with which we ask the question, "How are you?" when passing an acquaintance, or even a stranger. In theory, it's a great question. It has the potential to gain true insight into the life of another; insights that may be used to build a friendship, offer a helping hand, or share a word of encouragement.

However, the asking of this question has become nothing more than a formality. And so have its answers. "Fine thanks." "I'm great...how 'bout you?" Never mind the pain in our marriage. Forget about the fear of the pending test results or the financial stress of being unemployed. We give brief, predictable answers because that's what the world wants to hear.

People want to hear that we are good, great, or even awesome. We hide our concerns and struggles because we don't want others to think less of us. Whether we are five or fifty, we don't want our deficiencies to show because we want everyone to believe that we have it all together.

When I was young, boys were taught to act tough. We learned that we weren't supposed to cry when we fell off our bikes or scraped our knees. We learned to buck-up because the world doesn't want weak boys. The only time it was okay for us to cry was in sporting endeavors. Otherwise, we were to maintain a tough exterior at all times.

Early in life, boys and girls alike learn to be very selective about who sees their weaknesses. When a child gets injured the reaction is likely to be far more dramatic if Mom is the only witness than if the child is on the playground with friends. Why? We let Mom hear us wail because she will love us despite our failures, but we act tough for our friends so they won't laugh at us or think we're stupid for getting hurt. We decide early in life that it's easier to hide our deficiencies than to risk being judged for them.

Have you ever wanted to say how you really felt, but simply said *fine*? Have you ever said *yes*, even though you wanted to say *no*? Do you listen to different types of music depending on who is around you? Do you attend certain activities simply to fit in? By the way, these are not just questions for kids. They are questions for adults, too.

Our lives become consumed with attending the *right* social gatherings, driving the *right* vehicles, and having the *right* jobs. We want our kids to act mature and achieve good grades so that people will think that we are good parents. We learn that it is safer to live socially acceptable, politically correct lives than to risk being unpopular. And we learn to judge our success by the world's standards. How much *power* do I have? How much *prestige* do I have? How many *possessions* have I accumulated?

When I am introduced as the founder and president of MVP Leadership, it gives me a sense of accomplishment. When I ran for governor, I developed a great sense of prestige.

When Darla and I had our new home built, it was a possession of which we were very proud. In many ways, I have allowed things like these to define me. As a matter of fact, I *like* having these things define me because I want people to think highly of me. I want them to know me by my success, not by failures or mediocrity.

To some degree, it matters to each of us what other people think. It matters what others think of our careers and our social circles. It matters what others think of our spouses and our kids. It matters what others think of our vehicles and the positions we hold in the community. It matters. And it causes us to become masters of disguise, wearing whatever mask the situation dictates. We accumulate a complex collection of masks, each one designed to protect the core of who we really are. Each one designed to showcase our power, prestige, or possessions so that our inadequacies will remain neatly tucked away.

I habitually wore masks for many years. When in the business arena, I sported the mask of a leader. At church, I sported the mask of godly husband and father. When coaching a basketball game, I sported the mask of a motivator. In fact, I became an expert at masquerading and was quite content with my mask collection until Lucas entered our lives.

Lucas has a head that is much larger than normal. His hair is patchy in places and he has very low muscle tone. Lucas has frequent seizures. He cries out when he's happy and he cries out when he's sad. There is no hiding his disabilities, his deficiencies. No matter the party he attends or the home he visits, Lucas is Lucas.

The beauty of Lucas is that he never wears masks. He will cry out when it is inappropriate to cry out. He will laugh when it is inappropriate to laugh. He will clap when it is inappropriate to clap. And he will demand an emergency helicopter ride even when it disrupts our lives. He is real. He doesn't pretend to think or feel a particular way in order to please others. He doesn't even know how to pretend. That is what makes him so attractive to me. He defines authenticity.

From the time Lucas was born, people have wanted to know how we are doing and how Lucas is doing. We are often asked the habitual question, "How are you?" Although we appreciate the inquiries, we realize that most people don't really want to take the time necessary to hear the details of our life with Lucas.

For more than a year we gave tidy answers, ones that could be given in ten seconds or less and always ensured the comfort of those inquiring. As time passed, though, I had a growing desire to give candid answers, to be authentic. In the fall of 1994, we allowed our local newspaper to do a front-page story about Lucas' World. We talked very openly about the impact Lucas' life was having on Hans and Josh. We talked about our hopes and dreams for Lucas, and how Darla and I felt when he was diagnosed with Partial Pachygyria Lissencephaly. The opportunity to be authentic was refreshing; finally able to give the lengthy, honest, and sometimes uncomfortable answers to the question, "How are you doing?"

Lucas was born two days after the birth of Jacob, Darla's nephew. Jake gave us an immediate means of comparison, a constant reminder of the expectation for boys Lucas' age. Jake was born healthy. He has grown to be a great kid with a charming personality. He is extremely competitive and has won awards at several basketball camps. We realized right away that Lucas would never measure up to Jake. Not only was it disheartening to compare the two, I am convinced that it was a disservice to Lucas, to Darla and me, and even to Jake to do so.

That is why when we were interviewed for the newspaper article, I talked about the way we had come to assess Lucas' progress. Early in his life, we stopped comparing him to other children his age and began measuring him to the likes of a cross-country runner. A good cross-country runner understands that he is running every race against himself. His success depends on meeting and improving his own best times.

We began comparing Lucas to Lucas. Is he beating his personal best? Is he attaining that which he is able to attain according to the abilities God has given him?

When Lucas was seven years old we attended a staffing that I will never forget. We sat around a table with several professionals prepared to give their assessments of our son. They took turns, each one telling us the age level Lucas had reached in a particular category. They systematically discussed his physical and cognitive development. What struck me with disapproval was the fact that not one of them even mentioned our son's capacity for contentment. Not one of them addressed his level of happiness. Parents want to know that their children are happy. We want our children to feel fulfilled, to find success according to their unique God-given talents and gifts. Nobody was telling me that Lucas was happy.

I waited for them to go through their extensive studies before calling a proverbial time out. I explained that I care deeply about his progress, but more importantly, I want to know that he is happy. I asked them if there was some sort of happiness continuum.

Lucas will never be a rocket scientist. He will never walk and, unless there is a miracle, he will never talk. Even though we would love for that to happen, we are convinced it won't and I wanted this room of professionals to understand that his emotional well-being is our greatest concern. At that moment, charts and graphs measuring Lucas' progress against societal standards seemed cold and senseless.

It felt as though they were judging his worth according to the way he stacked up against others. They were forcing him to wear a mask, a mask that said, "I'm not so bad because I'm doing better than 50% of kids like me." It frustrated me because it threatened the very thing that I love about Lucas. He is real, incapable of pretending, and he never wears masks. He is who he is. He is who God created him to be. Lucas has taught me to throw out my collection of masks and to be real. He has taught me to focus on improving my personal best and challenged me to strive for the approval of the One who created me rather than spending my time and energy seeking the approval of men.

In 1 Thessalonians 2:4-6, Paul writes, "We are not

trying to please men but God, who tests our hearts. You know we never used flattery, nor did we put on a mask to cover up greed – God is our witness. We were not looking for praise from men." Paul wasn't interested in wearing a mask to improve his reputation or to gain the praises of people. He simply wanted to please God.

When our oldest son, Hans, was a junior in high school, I took him to a men's conference in Des Moines, which happened to take place in the same arena as the annual state basketball tournaments. As we left the event Friday night, he expressed how much he would love to return to that arena to play a tournament game with his team. Hans is a very good ball player. People love to watch him. He is often highlighted on the sports page for his exceptional offensive performance and was the only junior to be elected first-team, all-conference in 2005.

With this type of success, I knew it would be natural for him to focus on the glory and begin playing for the cheers of the crowd. His comments provided me the perfect opportunity to discuss the importance of seeking God's approval above all else. I simply said, "Hans, I don't care how many people show up to watch you play, or how many cameras are on you, stay narrowly focused on playing for an audience of One. Play for God's approval, not the approval of your coach. Play for God's pleasure, not your mom's and mine. Play for God, not your peers. He is the One that gave you the talent and resolve to play the game with excellence. Play it for Him."

The movie *Chariots of Fire*[3] tells the true story of Olympic runner Eric Liddell. When sharing his passion for running, Liddell says, "I believe that God made me for a purpose, but he also made me fast and when I run, I feel God's pleasure." He recognized the source of his talent and he understood the concept of playing for an audience of One.

When Duke basketball guard, J.J. Redick, was interviewed[4] about his near-perfect free throw record, he described his technique step-by-step: Step to the line, square-up the body, see the hoop, dribble once, spin the ball, dribble once more, spin the ball, recite Philippians 4:13 "I can do all things through Christ who gives me strength," and shoot. What a testimony of authenticity. Redick wasn't afraid to remove the mask of stud athlete and admit, on national television, that he depends on God for his strength.

Trying to please *people* can make your life incredibly complicated. Everyone you come into contact with has a different standard of success and a different opinion of how to achieve it. But living only for God's pleasure, simplifies your life and give you the freedom to take risks. He already knows your deficiencies, yet loves you as though you are perfect. His opinion of you is not formed according to your power, prestige, or possessions, so you can take risks without the fear of rejection.

When I left Sheldon High School to go to Opportunities Unlimited, my dad, who is generally supportive of my life decisions, thought I was crazy. The first time I told Darla I wanted to run for governor, she had three words for me, and they weren't "I love you." They were, "Are you nuts!" In fact, there were many who questioned that decision and told me

I simply couldn't, and shouldn't, do it. But I was, and remain, determined to play for an audience of One.

When you feel a particular call placed on your heart, and you are sincere about solely pleasing the Lord, then you leave a job that makes sense and a position that is respected, and you take a flier. You risk your reputation, and you campaign for a political office that most people say is impossible to attain. Even if the outcome seems like a failure in the eyes of the world, I have achieved success if I have truly acted in obedience, seeking to please the Lord.

Too often, the fear of failure holds us captive. We don't want to look foolish, so we don't take risks that we believe God wants us to take. But His kingdom is far more important than what other people think of us and true success is not about living up to the world's standards. True success is about knowing the living God. When you understand your identity as a child of the King, your politically correct reputation becomes far less significant and you are able to boldly pursue His pleasure.

How do you please Him? You throw away your masks and you risk being real. You risk looking foolish. You develop a new measure of success, realizing that the One within you is far more important than those around you. And you begin to play for an audience of One; playing hard in spite of obstacles, playing hard in spite of popular opinion, and never underestimating the Spirit of God. He is the one that gives you the strength to be authentic, to put aside cheap imitations and be the person that He created you to be.

Dear Lucas,

Do you ever wonder or care what people think about you? I know, dumb question. I can tell by your actions that you really don't care.

Throwing your cup after drinking its contents doesn't "fly" in most social circles. Sharing your chosen emotion with a multipitched scream is quite the attention getter in any setting. Closing your eyes and pretending to sleep while someone is trying desperately to entertain you has an immediate and humbling effect. And, my personal favorite, laughing uncontrollably while filling your pants takes the meaning of "manhood" to a whole new level.

Mom is quick to tell me not to encourage these behaviors. I agree you have areas that may need some brushing up, but I must admit that I love your authenticity. It's a breath of fresh air (save the filling the pants while laughing stunt) in a stuffy society where people take themselves, their dress, their position, and their words way too seriously.

You are you all the time. When you're happy, people know you're happy. When you're mad or sad, they know you're mad or sad. When you're grumpy and tired, your emotions say you are grumpy and tired. When you're excited to see us, or listen to a song, or go for a ride, every stitch of your demeanor says you're excited. You don't harbor or display any false emotions. You are

Lucas...crystal clear...100% authentic...all the time.

My world encourages the use of masks and the art of spin. You have taught me to be real. Believe me, I'm not as real as you are, but I'm gaining. I'm learning to take myself and my inadequacies less seriously and I love you for that.

I love you for who you are. Lucas, you are beautiful all the time. You were knit together in Mom's womb by our Father in Heaven and every one of your days was ordained for you before you were even born. There is only one you and you never try to hide who you really are by wearing a socially acceptable mask.

Thank you for simply being you. I love you, kid!

You Are Never Alone

For eleven years I was surrounded by high school students, teachers, and parents. I loved it. For me, the greatest reward of serving as an educator, whether in the classroom or as a principal, was experiencing people. Young or old, people inspire me.

Following my career in education I became a public speaker, leading teacher in-services, student assemblies, business seminars, and working with various corporate boards. These are opportunities that I still have today. I love it. It is inspiring when you have the opportunity to touch people's lives, if only for a moment.

When I entered the political world as a candidate for governor, I spent hundreds of hours visiting communities across Iowa, visiting with citizens and leaders. I loved it. It was great fun experiencing different cultures within the same state, talking with people about their concerns, and participating in their celebrations - networking, networking, networking to build my team.

My entire adult life has been about people. I have chosen careers and volunteer efforts that have kept me surrounded with people of all ages, social and economic backgrounds, and political positions. I love being with people.

There have been times in my life, though, when I have been with literally hundreds of people yet I've felt drastically alone. It is truly a paradox.

I have come to realize that my feelings of loneliness

have had much less to do with the number of people around me and much more to do with who is controlling my life.

You've surely heard the saying, "There's power in numbers." True. You've heard it said, "Many hands make light work." True again. But, you've also heard, "Too many cooks spoil the broth." The very best plans will turn to chaos unless there is someone leading; a leader that is skilled at blending individual talents to fulfill a compelling vision.

We human beings love to be in control, spending excessive amounts of time and energy on that which benefits our own desires. Don't give me the copilot seat, I'll fly this plane!

I like 'piloting' my own life because it feels good to be in control. If you are honest with yourself, you like it too. We enjoy controlling our own agenda as long as everything is going smoothly.

However, flying without a pilot's license can be fatal.

When on the campaign trail, I have had many opportunities to fill the copilot's chair of private aircraft and observe the intricacies of flying. The instrument panel is like a living object, with various gauges constantly moving and changing. Through the headsets, come frequent air tower communications that may or may not be intended for your aircraft. And then there are the manuals and maps throughout the cockpit.

As much as I would love to fly the plane, and as often as I've been the passenger, putting me in the pilot seat would surely end in disaster. If I want to get to my destination alive, I need to have a pilot that understands where we came from, where we're going, and how to get there.

Just as a successful flight requires a skilled pilot, a successful life requires a God who understands where we came from, where we need to go, and how to get us there. It requires us to surrender control and submit to His agenda, putting our own ambitions aside. We must let God be our pilot.

When I insist on taking the pilot seat, I find myself exhausted; attempting to do what I am not qualified to do. But moving to my rightful place as copilot removes the pressure. It puts God in charge, and knowing that I'm not alone returns the bounce to my step.

Even so, there are times when I grasp for control with all my might...fiercely determined to fly my plane. It is at these times, fighting a losing battle for control, when I feel desperately alone. Countless times, when Lucas has hung in the balance between life and death, I've been left feeling powerless and alone.

One evening, Darla was working in the kitchen, holding Lucas, while Hans, Josh, and I visited at the kitchen table. When Darla reached to retrieve a glass from the cupboard she heard Lucas take in a long, deep breath. She expected, of course, to hear it followed by an equal exhale, but one never came. She recalls looking down at him, lying in her arms, and realizing that he had stopped breathing. Immediately, she called to me for help. I scooped him up and ran to the living room. Darla was right behind me. When I put Lucas on the floor to begin rescue breathing him, Darla knelt down beside us, close to hysteria. Hans and Josh, a kindergartener and a preschooler, looked on as their brother's life was slipping away right in front of their eyes.

Grabbing the phone, I told Hans to dial 9-1-1. I remember tilting Lucas' head back, putting my mouth over his, and reciting the steps in my mind that I had learned in CPR training. I never thought I'd have to use that training, especially on my own son, but it would be the first of many times. At that moment, clutching his tiny body and breathing into his mouth, I felt powerless. No matter the method I used or how well I performed it, I was incapable of making him respond.

I remember Darla regaining her composure. I remember telling Hans and Josh to run to the front yard and watch for the ambulance. They needed to leave the room because I didn't want them to see their little brother die on the living room floor. I was relying solely on CPR training and human efforts for security, yet feeling completely powerless and alone.

In August of 1995, Lucas was two years old. Darla and I decided to attend the Lissencephaly Network Conference in Boston which would help to build our knowledge of Lucas' condition and build a network of support. We took all three boys and since they would outnumber us, we decided to beef up the troops by bringing a caregiver along.

The doctor had given us a prescription for Lucas that was supposed to help him better handle the flight to Boston. Although the flight went okay, we became aware throughout the day that something wasn't quite right. After arriving in Boston, we decided to take Lucas to the emergency room.

We were very familiar with emergency room visits, but the members of the medical staff of this particular hospital were not familiar with Lucas. They tried relentlessly to establish an IV line, eventually getting it done. But it wasn't long before the line blew and they had to repeat the whole painful process; painful for Lucas to experience, painful for us to watch. He absolutely looked like a pin cushion. Darla pleaded with the medical staff to insert the line in his neck where his veins are much more visible, but they refused.

They observed Lucas for a couple of days and once he was released, we took him to the conference with us. By lunchtime he had become completely lethargic, not eating or drinking, and we were concerned. The fun family trip and wonderful learning experience that we had anticipated was turning into a series of worry and disappointment.

Reluctantly, but without another option, we returned to the emergency room. This time, Darla insisted that they leave his arms and legs alone. She was so insistent, in fact, that the doctor asked us to leave the room while the medical team tried to establish a line in his neck. Because it was a teaching hospital, there were several interns tending to him, and mistakes were being made that could have been avoided. It was exasperating to watch and our frustration was obvious to the attending physician, so obvious, that he didn't want us in the room.

We were overwhelmed with emotion. We had watched our son suffer as he endured a painful, repetitive procedure that seemed futile to us...while all along having the knowledge and instinct to remedy the situation. We were helpless, full of frustration and anger. As we left the emergency room and entered the elevator, Darla looked at me and said the words that captured my sentiment as well, "There is no God."

We felt so alone. If there is a God, why would he put Lucas through that! He hadn't done anything wrong and he didn't deserve any of it. He wasn't obnoxious, defiant, or naughty. He was incapable of willful sins. If there is a God, surely he would have rescued Lucas from all the ugliness. Surely he would have taken him home to Heaven where his suffering would be over. Surely he could have healed him so that he wouldn't have had to endure the pain.

We stood silent in the elevator. When the doors opened, Darla went one way and I went the other. We needed time apart. And the ironic thing is that we both used that time apart to pray to the God whose existence we had just denied.

After awhile, we returned to the elevator. In the midst of an emotional embrace, we both confessed that there is indeed a God and that He is the only one with the strength to get us, and Lucas, through these painful times. When we admitted that we were powerless and surrendered control, He carried us through.

When Lucas was six years old, Darla and I reached the very difficult decision to seek full time care for him. We were struggling to adequately meet his needs at home while still caring for his three brothers, so we admitted him to Children's Care Hospital and School (CCHS) in Sioux Falls, South Dakota.

You've heard of empty nest syndrome. So had we. But the sorrow and anxiety a parent experiences when an adult child goes to college or gets married doesn't compare to the discomfort of leaving a six-year-old in the hands of others, walking away knowing that he is alone.

The most frustrating emotion that Darla and I experienced during those first few days was that of guilt...not the guilt of leaving him, but the guilt of feeling relieved. We felt so good about the decision, knowing that it was a wonderful facility and that he would be well cared for according to his unique needs.

Returning home to Sioux City, we experienced a full night of sleep. Before, we had an arrangement that Darla would get up in the night with the baby, Logan, because her body was better equipped to meet his demands, and I would get up with Lucas. Whether summoned by cries or monitor alarms, when Lucas had a need in the night I would get up to be with him. Many mornings, he would wake up very early. So in an effort to keep the rest of the family from being disturbed, I would put Lucas into one of our vehicles and we would take a morning cruise (something he still loves to this day).

The decrease in demands after moving Lucas to CCHS was refreshing, but there were also times during the separation process that we felt desperately alone, questioning our decision. We were depending on other people to raise the son that God entrusted to us, and that was a difficult reality at times. Even now, years later, we experience moments of guilt as we kiss Lucas goodbye and make the drive back to Sioux City, but we believe wholeheartedly that we are doing what is best for him. And we know that God is with him. Deuteronomy 31:8 promises, "The Lord himself goes before you and will be with you; *he will never leave you* nor forsake you."

Despite the many difficult decisions and emergency situations we have had with Lucas, our loneliest moments came in the spring of 2004, when he was scheduled for full spinal fusion surgery at the University of Iowa Hospital. The doctor explained that it would be a long surgery, about six hours, and that Lucas would lose nearly 60% of his blood. The discs in his back would be removed, allowing the spine to collapse, and then they would strategically place rods along the spine until it was straightened. A mere cold can send Lucas into seizures, resulting in life or death situations, so we knew that this surgery was going to be a major event. And we felt very alone.

On Wednesday, April 6, Darla and I took Lucas to Iowa City for his surgery. After checking into our hotel room, the three of us laid on the bed together and read Psalm 139:

O Lord, you have searched me and you know me. You know when I sit and when I rise; you perceive my thoughts from afar. You discern my going out and my lying down; you are familiar with all my ways. Before a word is on my tongue you know it completely...
Where can I go from your Spirit? Where can I flee from your presence? If I go up to the heavens, you are there; if I make my bed in the depths, you are there. If I rise on the wings of the dawn, if I settle on the far side of the sea, even there your hand will guide me; your right hand will hold me fast.

If I say, "Surely the darkness will hide me and the light become night around me," even the darkness will not be dark to you; the night will shine like the day, for darkness is as light to you.

*For you created my inmost being; you knit me
together in my mother's womb. I praise you
because I am fearfully and wonderfully made;
your works are wonderful, I know that full well.
My frame was not hidden from you when I was
made in the secret place. When I was woven
together in the depths of the earth, your eyes saw
my unformed body. All the days ordained for me
were written in your book before one of them
came to be.*

We understood the severity of Lucas' surgery, and knew
that these could be his last days. Because I believe the only
way to Heaven is through Christ's sacrifice, my father's heart
was burdened for Lucas' salvation.

After reading Psalm 139, we prayed. We thanked God
that we can't ever flee from His presence and that He knows
the number of our days. We thanked God for the gift of Lucas.
We prayed that God would hold Lucas in His arms through
the surgery. And we prayed a very personal prayer on behalf
of Lucas, receiving Christ's gift of eternal life. Although Lucas
couldn't nod in agreement or say the words, we know that God
answered that prayer. Those intimate moments gave Darla and
me great comfort as we sent Lucas into surgery.

The surgery went as expected, but Lucas battled to
recover for two months. Many of his days were spent in the
intensive care unit. Many were spent in, or near, critical condition. We were required to make many difficult decisions during

those months and saw his temperature reach 107 degrees. It was a day-to-day struggle, with many fearful moments.

At one point, Lucas was even taken back into surgery. The doctors needed to irrigate his incision because he had developed a staph infection. With a sky-high fever and extended periods of unconsciousness, we thought we were going to lose him. Darla and I prayed for God's will to be done, but we also prayed, if it was his time, that God would take Lucas quickly, while he was at peace under the anesthetic.

As we sat in the surgical waiting room, Darla and I began planning a funeral for our son. In a strange way, I hoped that for Lucas. He deserved to be whole and happy. He deserved to see Christ's face and to feel the embrace of a Savior who also endured suffering through no guilt of his own. I just wanted his suffering to be over. Spending time in prayer truly brought us peace. In fact, after planning and praying, Darla wrapped herself up in Lucas' Scooby-Do blanket and put her head on my shoulder. I rested my head on hers and we both fell asleep.

Every time I've tried to be my own pilot, trying to make sense of chaos and control circumstances, I am left feeling fatigued and alone. But every time that I've stayed purposely in my copilot seat, turning my focus to prayer and the truth in God's word, I've found peace. Every time. Surrendering control and submitting to God's perfect will floods my soul with comfort and replaces feelings of loneliness with a powerful awareness that I am never alone. He never leaves. Even when I try to escape His presence, He's there.

I sometimes wear a silver chain that has a shield hanging from it. On the back of the shield, these words are engraved: "Be strong and courageous. Do not be terrified; do not be discouraged, for the Lord your God will be with you wherever you go" (Joshua 1:9b).

Psalm 139, the one that we read to Lucas before his surgery, assures us that we cannot flee from God's presence. If you go up to the heavens, He is there. If you make your bed in the depths, He is there. If you go into a surgical room without your mom and dad, He is there. If you live at a full time care facility away from your family, He is there. If you stand in your living room watching your son's life slipping away, He is there. If you see your child suffering, crying out in pain, He is there.

What situations are you dealing with today that have made you feel powerless and alone? Get out of the pilot seat, cease your efforts for control, and allow God to navigate your life. He is there for you and He longs to see the bounce return to your step and a sparkle in your eye.

I still love to be surrounded by people. That hasn't changed. But I've learned that speaking at big events and leading teams of executives in board room discussions cannot be the source of my security. Lucas, a kid who lives a life of solitude, has taught me that security is found simply in knowing that we are never alone. He has taught me the precious truth that when life brings situations beyond our control and heartache beyond reason, God is always there to see us through.

Dear Lucas,

Every time you go "code blue", Mom and I, along with anyone else in the room, go "code scared to death." I'm sure you see the fear in our eyes and hear the fear in our voices. I'm sure that our fear does nothing to comfort you as you struggle to hold on to life and I'm sorry for that.

I know you feel alone and frightened each time you enter a seizure or an unstable medical condition. I see the fear in your eyes, too. I wish so much that I could say just the right words or do just the right thing to take your fear away. But, if I were you, I would be scared too.

God tells us in His Word to "Be strong and courageous. Do not be terrified; do not be discouraged..." (Joshua 1:9). Your fight for life has proven over and over again that God's instruction is easier said than done. When you stop breathing, you're scared. When you hear an ambulance coming and you know it's coming for you, you're scared. When you see needles being prepared...you're scared.

The reason God tells you "do not be afraid" is because He is with you...always. He will never leave you, Lucas. I wish I could tell you that God will never let you hurt again, but I can't. The only promise I can make is that He loves you, He loves your mom and me, and He will never let us face life's struggles alone.

Even though I have run both to and from God

during your medical emergencies, He has never moved. Every time I have been filled with fear, afraid of losing you, God's love and embrace has been evident.

If we could, Mom and I would be with you constantly, but we simply can't. So, my fervent prayer for you is that you will feel the power of God's love and embrace all the time...every minute of every day.

Never forget, Lucas, that you will never be alone. God's love, Mom's love, and my love are with you always.

Thank God for Moms

Darla and I had our first date on Friday, December 12, 1980. She is still impressed that I recall the exact date considering the fact that men don't have the best track record of remembering such details, but the reason is very simple. I remember it in detail because it was the day that I found the perfect woman – or at least the perfect woman for me. We were both seniors in high school and she was beautiful. Our high school basketball team had a game that night and she was going to the game to watch me play. When I picked her up that evening, she hoarsely explained that she had a case of laryngitis. I remember thinking that life doesn't get much better than this: a beautiful girl, who can't talk, is accompanying me to my basketball game. It was perfect.

Darla and I were quite different from one another. She was a great student. She loved to read. She studied hard. She was on the honor roll. When her parents needed to issue her a punishment, they restricted her reading time. Now if my parents would have used the same method of punishment, I would have been all for it. Sign me up, Mom and Dad. When I mess up, don't let me read for two or three days, or better yet, two or three months!

Darla was awarded academic scholarships, music scholarships, presidential scholarships, and she went on to graduate summa cum laude from Northwestern College. Darla and I shared the last name Vander Plaats by the time of our college graduation, married for nearly two years, so when they announced the graduates in alphabetical order, the D in Darla came before the R in Robert. They announced Darla's name, followed by the title of summa cum laude, and I remember thinking, "What did they just call her?" Of course, when they announced my name, it was simply Robert L. Vander Plaats. End of introduction.

Darla was focused on developing her career. She was going to take the accounting profession by storm, passing the entire CPA exam on her first try. Again, I saw her as the perfect woman: smart, beautiful, great earning potential, yet she always allowed me to believe that I was the leader of our home. She was supportive of my career as a teacher and coach, knowing that she would be the primary breadwinner.

But an amazing transition took place on February 23, 1988, with the birth of our first child, Hans. All of the sudden we were both experiencing the emotions of parenthood. Darla took a long sabbatical from her career and when the time came to return, she struggled in her search to find a caregiver for Hans. Once she selected someone, it was incredibly difficult for Darla to put our baby in someone else's arms each morning on her way to the office. Her priorities had shifted dramatically and her career was no longer her primary focus. What mattered more was being a mom.

Three years later, along came our second son, Josh. Up to that point, Darla remained engaged as a CPA with an accounting firm and I was still teaching and coaching, while pursuing my master's degree and running a landscaping business.

With the birth of Josh, Darla was convinced that it was time for her to leave her career and focus on raising our sons.

It was a difficult decision, but we both believe that moms and dads should be the primary caregivers whenever possible. Trusting God to provide for our financial needs, we made the decision for Darla to become a stay-at-home mom.

Soon after making that decision, I accepted an offer to become a high school principal. The position came with a larger salary and better benefits, making it easier for Darla to stay at home. Although it was an adjustment, we settled into the idea that Darla would be a full time mom and I would be the primary breadwinner. It was a much different life than we had envisioned back in college, but I believe it was God's way of preparing us for the birth of Lucas.

He knew that Lucas would require focused attention. If Lucas had been born into a different situation, he may not have survived. But the love, care, and abundant time that Darla has been able to provide is likely the reason he as progressed to where he is today.

Stepping away from her career didn't rob Darla of her intelligence or squelch her ability to learn things quickly. In fact, she employed her love for learning to study Lucas' diagnosis, procedures, and medications. She has become articulate with the medical community, able to communicate with doctors and nurses regarding Lucas' needs. I have seen her remain poised, offering lifesaving information in the midst of emergency situations.

When the medical community has been willing to work with us, particularly Darla, Lucas has been spared unnecessary and painful procedures. His quality of care has been enhanced through Darla's input, and not only through her knowledge of the facts, but through her instinct...her mother's intuition.

When Lucas was recovering from full spinal fusion surgery, I became acutely aware of the difference between doctors and moms.

Lucas had been on a ventilator following surgery and when they extabated him, he went into severe distress. The room filled immediately with medical professionals employing their best efforts to stabilize him, but he was unresponsive. It was Darla that made the suggestion that would ultimately save his life. She watched nervously as the professionals worked on him without result, finally saying, "Let's give him a bolus of Ativan so that we will know if his issue is seizure related or if it's something else." Without hesitation, without committees, and without questions the doctor in charge followed Darla's advice and Lucas responded exactly as she predicted. As the doctor left the intensive care room that day, he looked at my dad and said, "Thank God for moms."

Doctors are intensely educated individuals with high IQs and thousands of hours of experience. They stay up-to-date on research and use proven methods to save lives every day. They deserve our respect and our thanks.

Moms, on the other hand, may not have medical degrees or teaching certificates. They may not be wise according to the world's standards, but they have an uncanny awareness of what their children need. 1 Corinthians 1:27 says, "But God chose the foolish things of this world to shame the wise... the weak things of this world to shame the strong." I believe that this passage is teaching us to value instinct over intellect; making a lifesaving judgment call without opening a textbook...saying or doing exactly what needs to be said or done, void of degrees or certificates.

Lucas is incredibly blessed to have a mom that absorbs knowledge quickly and is tireless in pursuing information about his condition, advocating for him in a way that is respected by the medical community. But more important, is Darla's keen awareness of what is best for him simply because she's his mom.

A most popular scripture passage for Mother's Day sermons is Chapter 31 of Proverbs. It's great material for a touching lesson, but even more powerful has been the opportunity to see those verses lived out in the life of Darla.

Proverbs 31:11-12 says, "Her husband has full confidence in her and lacks nothing of value. She brings him good, not harm..." Darla embodies these verses, always giving me her full support in major life decisions. And it is that support which has made me appreciate her character. She supported my career as a teacher and coach and was excited when I had the opportunity to become a high school principal. While in the midst of raising three young children, one with severe disabilities, she supported my decision to leave the security of the public school system and become the president and CEO of an ailing nonprofit organization. She even supported my campaign for governor, despite the overwhelming odds and my extensive travel schedule.

Proverbs 31 also celebrates a woman's hard work and the care she gives to her family saying, "She sets about her work vigorously...She watches over the affairs of her household and does not eat the bread of idleness." Again, I see this in

Darla. I am inspired by the selfless attention that she devotes to our family. Not only does she give specialized care to Lucas, but she invests an incredible amount of time and energy into the lives of Hans, Josh and Logan. When on the campaign trail, Darla was asked about her potential agenda as the state's First Lady. She confidently answered, "If I'm provided the opportunity to be your First Lady, my first role will be as First Mom." It made me wish for a greater number of politically involved parents willing to commit first to their families, and then to their constituents.

Proverbs 31:20 talks about service and Darla loves to serve. She possesses many talents, yet has a beautiful spirit of humility. She serves our church with her musical gift, playing the piano and organ. She serves young moms in the Mothers of Preschoolers program. She serves the boys' schools, working in elementary classrooms and facilitating high school fundraisers. If she knows of an unmet need, she seeks to serve. I love that about her because she's teaching our sons to think of others above themselves.

She is also teaching them about integrity. Verses 25-26 say, "She is clothed with strength and dignity...She speaks with wisdom, and faithful instruction is on her tongue." Anyone who knows Darla recognizes her strength of character and the wisdom with which she speaks. She has modeled the character of Christ to our children, and to me. In large part, it is Darla's standard of integrity that inspired me to run a positive political campaign. When strategists were advising us to attack, we stayed committed to giving people something to vote *for* not something to vote *against*. Why? Because our boys were watching and they were learning how to relate to the world around them.

Although Darla is a beautiful woman on the outside, it is her inner beauty that has captured my heart. Verse 30 says, "Charm is deceptive, and beauty is fleeting; but a woman who fears the Lord is to be praised." Darla seeks the Lord with passion. He is her first love, and that is what makes her truly beautiful.

Finally, Proverbs 31 recognizes the praise that is due to a woman of noble character, "Her children arise and call her blessed; her husband also, and he praises her." The boys and I are far from perfect in the way we uphold Darla, failing often to give her the honor that she deserves. But we absolutely adore her for the wife, mother, and friend that she is to us and for the inspiration she gives us to be better men.

The Pharisees were the religious men of Jesus' day, well-educated in biblical facts. They knew the law, and were tenacious in promoting it...every "i" dotted, every "t" crossed. The Pharisees focused on matters of the intellect. But Jesus rocked their system by speaking of compassion and forgiveness. He promoted servanthood and the practice of examining your own actions rather than judging the actions of others. He focused on matters of the heart.

A mother's worth can't be measured academically. Her worth doesn't lie within her intellect, but within the fabric of her soul. It lies in the instinctive decisions that she makes on behalf of her family, not in the knowledge accumulated from textbooks.

So our society should sincerely thank the professionals

for their expertise. We need to thank teachers for instructing our children in mathematics, the sciences, and the arts. We need to thank doctors and nurses for the countless hours that they've spent perfecting their skills in order to save lives and provide relief from strep throat and diaper rash. We need to appreciate the significance that knowledge and technology have in our society.

But more than that, we need to celebrate moms, who teach us the stuff of life that isn't contained in the classroom. We need to celebrate their love, and care, and beauty. And we need to celebrate the wisdom that they impart to their children, and on behalf of their children; wisdom that is born within the heart of a mother when she looks upon the face of her son or daughter, knowing that she has the privilege and responsibility of commissioning the next generation.

As I have observed Darla's love and care for Lucas, it has both humbled and inspired me. She will never receive a diploma for her performance as his mother, never hear him say the words *thank you* or *I love you,* but she remains passionate in her love for him and diligent in her duty to him. I believe it's a beautiful picture of what God intended moms to be. Not perfect. Not famous. Not even summa cum laude...just lovers of their children...no matter what. And in the words of Lucas' doctor, "Thank God for Moms!"

Dear Lucas,

You have a special mom. I've known she's a special person for a long time, but your birth allowed me to see her beauty in a new way. She loves you very much.

Your mom went through a lot when she gave birth to you. But in typical style, her concern was not for herself, it was for you. She wanted to make sure that you were in good care. She even convinced the doctors to release her from the hospital early so she could be with you.

I don't believe you would be alive today had you been born to someone besides your mother. She has startled the medical community and the experts with her knowledge and instincts for your care. What makes her care so special is that it is completely motivated by her love for you.

The decision to put you in someone else's care was clearly the toughest decision your mom and I have ever made. It was painful, to say the least. It still pains us to leave for home after our visits with you. And we only find peace because we know it is God's best for you and our family. I hope you understand.

I know you love it when we visit. My greatest pleasure during our times together is watching the bond between you and Mom. You both escape the monotony and struggles of this world when you're together. Mom's embrace, her songs, and her total presence reveal her love for you and her thanks to God. Seeing the way you *gaze into Mom's face with such love and contentment, is like seeing a masterpiece.*

Mom talks often of her desire to be in heaven with you. You better set aside a great deal of time for that heavenly reunion! She wants to experience all that has been missing from this life. She wants to see you walk, hear you sing, and to dance the streets of gold with you. What a day that will be! I hope you two won't mind if I join in!

I believe that God gives us moms to help us understand the tender love he has for us. Lucas, I hope that you thank God every day that He has given you such a beautiful picture of His love.

I love you, kid!

There Are Angels Among Us

In his book *Echoes of the Maggid*[5], Rabbi Paysch Krohn tells the story of a man who delivered a speech to the attendees of a fundraising dinner for his son's school, a school dedicated to serving children with disabilities.

After praising the school's dedicated staff, the father shocked the audience by crying out, "Where is the perfection in my son Shaya? Everything that God does is done with perfection. But my child cannot understand things as other children do. My child cannot remember facts and figures as other children do. Where is God's perfection?" His voice was anguished as he went on to tell the story of how God revealed his son's perfection.

One Sunday afternoon he and his son went on a walk by the local park where a group of boys were playing a game of baseball and Shaya wanted to play. Although he was obviously not athletic, one of the boys agreed to have him join their team since they were losing by six runs and the game was almost over. The father was ecstatic as he watched his son run onto the field.

By the bottom of the ninth inning, Shaya's team was losing by two runs, had two outs and bases loaded. And it was Shaya's turn to bat. The father tells of his nervousness as he watched his son awkwardly hold the bat and step up to the plate.

The pitcher stepped toward home plate and gently lobbed the ball to Shaya, who swung clumsily and missed. Trying to help, one of his teammates stepped behind Shaya and prepared to help him swing. Again, the pitcher stepped closer and tossed the ball. This time, Shaya hit the ball and it bounced across the ground to the pitcher.

The pitcher picked up the soft grounder and could easily have thrown the ball to the first baseman. Shaya would have been out and that would have ended the game.

Instead, the pitcher took the ball and threw it on a high arc to right field, far and wide beyond the first baseman's reach. Everyone started yelling, "Shaya, run to first! Shaya, run to first!" Never in his life had Shaya run to first.

He scampered down the baseline wide-eyed and startled. By the time he reached first base, the right fielder had the ball. He could have thrown the ball to the second baseman who would tag out Shaya, who was still running, but the right fielder understood what the pitcher's intentions were, so he threw the ball high and far over the third baseman's head, as everyone yelled, "Shaya, run to second! Shaya, run to second."

Shaya ran towards second base as the runners ahead of him deliriously circled the bases towards home. As Shaya reached second base, the opposing shortstop ran towards him, turned him towards the direction of third base and shouted, "Shaya, run to third!"

As Shaya rounded third, the boys from both teams ran behind him screaming, "Shaya, run home! Shaya, run home!"

Shaya ran home, stepped on home plate and all 18 boys lifted him on their shoulders and made him the hero, as he had just hit the "grand slam" and won the game for his team.

"That day," said the father who now had tears rolling down his face, "those 18 boys reached their level of perfection."

Every time I hear or relay the story of Shaya and his

father, tears roll down my face and emotion fills my voice. It is a rare picture of two teams, 18 boys, sacrificing their desire to win so that Shaya could experience what it felt like to be the hero. That is God's perfection!

Shaya's story has helped me to realize that God has displayed His perfection through Lucas time and time again, not through his disabilities but in how people have responded to his disabilities. You see, God's purpose for Lucas isn't for Lucas – it's for us. God's purpose for you and me isn't for you and me – it's for others. God's purpose for His children is to reveal His glory through the impact we have on others.

When Lucas attended preschool at Clark Elementary in Sioux City, his teacher would frequently take him to a third grade classroom so that the students could experience community with a child with disabilities. Throughout the school year, the kids grew comfortable with Lucas and truly enjoyed having him in their classroom.

In the spring of that year, while watching Josh play a little league baseball game against some of the students from Clark Elementary, we had the opportunity to see the result of a teacher's endeavor to show a group of students the importance of community.

We were sitting just outside the fence by first base and Lucas was on a blanket by our feet. We watched the pitch. Crack! The batter hit a line drive to the shortstop who promptly scooped up the ball and threw it to the first baseman. Unfortunately, the ball flew past the first baseman and hit the fence just in front of us. When the boy playing first base ran to retrieve the ball, his eyes glanced over to Lucas and he stopped, "Hey, Lucas. How you doin'?" By the time he picked up the ball and threw it to second, the runner was safe.

It was a precious reminder that people are more important than baseball. Friends are more important than winning. With a smile and a few kind words, this young first baseman showed that he valued Lucas above his own agenda. Jesus' entire ministry was about putting the cause above self; spreading the truth of God's love, power, and forgiveness even when it compromised His comfort, desires, and even His own life.

Many of my days have been spent teaching leadership strategies and working with business executives to maximize the potential of their organizations. We use words like character...integrity...excellence...leadership. At times these words can seem so distant, so intangible. It's hard to wholly define integrity, but you know it when you see it. It is difficult to adequately describe excellence, but you know it when you see it.

In the same way, the words *Christian community* can be elusive. Churches have become diligent in promoting Christian community, but many times the result is simply another program or committee. Although the concept of Christian community can be vague, you know it when you see it and we see it in the life of Jesus over and over again. He continually offered a helping hand and kind words to passersby, always compassionate to those with special needs. He took time to see people's hidden hurts and to love the unlovely.

The book of Matthew records several of Jesus' encounters with those in need. In Matthew 8:3, He shows compassion to a man with leprosy. We can assume that the man was covered with grotesque sores, yet Jesus "reached out his hand and touched the man" and the man was immediately healed. I wonder how long it had been since he had felt the touch of a friend.

Later in the same chapter, Jesus heals Peter's mother-in-law. "He touched her hand and the fever left her and she got up and began to wait on him" (Matthew 8:15). Again, he showed kindness through touch.

In Chapter 9, Jesus heals several people. He heals a paralyzed man and a woman who had been plagued with a bleeding disorder for much of her life. He brings a man's daughter back to life by touching her hand. He touches the eyes of two blind men and restores their sight. He restores speech to a mute man.

Jesus helped people over and over again, meeting their needs through the miraculous power of touch. He was compulsive about showing compassion. Why do you suppose the scriptures give so much attention to this aspect of our Savior? I don't believe that the purpose is to show what a great person He was, but to demonstrate how much He values servanthood. He left us an example to follow and His example pleads with us to humble ourselves and touch the lives of those in need.

He is the God of the universe. He could have performed mass healings in the blink of an eye, but He chose instead to come face to face with hurting people, to physically touch them. He didn't cut them a check and send them on their way. He didn't form a committee to look into their situation. He didn't give them a list of expectations or sign them up for a seminar. He found them in the streets, looked them in the eye, put His arm around them, and met their needs.

Paul tells us in Romans 15:4 that everything written in scripture is written to teach us. Matthew 12:18 and 20 tell us that Jesus was a servant, that "A bruised reed he will not break, and a smoldering wick he will not snuff out." Jesus consistently showed kindness to people with disabilities, and He expects the same from us. He never ignored the crippled or shamed the weak, He honored them. I believe He desires us to embrace the afflicted, those with special needs, allowing His glory, His perfection, to be revealed through our love for them.

The story of Ruth and Naomi, in the Old Testament, further demonstrates the essence of Christian community. Naomi becomes a widow while living away from the country where she was born and raised. Soon after her husband dies, both of Naomi's adult sons die also, leaving her alone with her two daughters-in-law, Orpah and Ruth. Naomi decides to return to her homeland, but instructs her daughters-in-law, whom she loves, to return to their mothers' homes where they might find new husbands. After many tears Orpah departs, but Ruth insists on accompanying her mother-in-law on the rugged and unknown journey.

In fact, Ruth speaks unswerving devotion and servanthood to Naomi, saying, "Don't urge me to leave you or to turn back from you. Where you go I will go, and where you stay I will stay. Your people will be my people and your God my God. Where you die I will die, and there I will be buried. May the Lord deal with me, be it ever so severely, if anything but death separates you and me" (Ruth 1:16-17). Wow, that's Christian community!

The opportunity to return to her family and have a husband was surely tempting and would certainly have provided more security, but Ruth had compassion for her mother-in-law and wanted to serve her. Ruth knew that Naomi was all alone and she wanted to care for her. She didn't give money or advice. She gave herself.

Lucas' birth was an instant call for Christian community. We greatly appreciated the phone calls, cards and casseroles, but we were in desperate need for someone to look us in the face, put their arms around us, and walk through the pains and needs of our days. And God sent us Ruth. Not the Ruth of the Old Testament, but *our* Ruth...Ruth Klein.

Soon after Lucas was born, I accepted a high school principal position. Ruth had been the secretary to the Sheldon High School principal for several years. So when I arrived she became my assistant. Ruth readily embraced me as the new principal, and she readily embraced Darla and our boys.

Not only was she accepting of us, but she began to model Christian community to us in a way that we had never experienced. It was more than saying, "I'm praying for you," although we knew she was. It was more than sending a plate of cookies home to the boys, though she did.

She modeled Christian community when she sat at the hospital with us, just in case we needed something. It was listening to our fears and frustrations, and not judging us for them. It was arriving on the doorstep in the middle of the night to watch Hans and Josh, so we could be in the emergency room with Lucas. It was holding Lucas in her arms when we were exhausted. It was rejoicing with us over good news, and weeping with us when we cried out, "Why?" It was, and continues to be, the willingness to give *herself* to us...to literally *touch* our lives.

She has made personal sacrifices in order to serve our family. When Darla and I moved to Sioux City with the boys, after I became the CEO of Opportunities Unlimited, Ruth was right there with us. She left her home in Sheldon and moved to Sioux City because she believed that God wanted her to continue serving our family. She served on the staff of OU as my assistant, and as the years have passed, Ruth has assisted us in our gubernatorial campaigns and with MVP Leadership.

We have been blessed immeasurably by Ruth. She loves our family and has always been there when we've needed her, but she has never asked anything in return. She hasn't done it for the praise or expected to receive a material reward. I believe that her biggest reward has been the love that she has received in return. She is blessed by the love she receives from Hans, Josh, Lucas and Logan. She is blessed by the love that she receives from Darla and me. I would agree with Shaya's dad, God's perfection is not found in Lucas' disabilities, but in the responses to Lucas' disabilities. His perfection has been displayed through people like Ruth.

I wrote a poem on Lucas' behalf to present as a gift to Ruth one Christmas. Nestled in a collage of photos, snapshots of Ruth and Lucas together, were these words:

Ruth is my special friend; I see her quite a bit,
we do many things together,
but sometimes we just clap and sit.
Ruth says that I am special; I believe her words are true,
my purposes in life may be many,
but one is to impact you.
Ruth makes me smile and brings my life great joy,
she sees my inner beauty and says
that I'm God's special boy.
Ruth is a part of my family,
just like my parents and brothers,
what makes Ruth so special is the
love that she gives to others.
When I'm with Ruth, there's a smile on my face,
she gives special feeling that cannot be replaced.
Ruth is like an angel; her kindness makes her shine,
one day she may be your friend,
I know she'll always be mine!

Although Lucas cannot talk, I believe that these words summarize his feeling for Ruth.

We need to BE Christian community. We need to reach out and touch people's lives. Meet them where they are, look them in the face, put our arm around their shoulders, and walk through their pains with them...whatever it takes. Cause above self. This is the life Christ modeled.

Walking this journey with Lucas has taught me that God calls us to follow His example of servanthood, and to have compassion for the weak and unlovely. We are so thankful for the "angels" God sends our way, to serve us and to show us compassion. Ruth has been our angel. She has modeled the spirit of Jesus to us through her hands, her words, her time, her emotion, her commitment, and her love. Experiencing her love and kindness inspires me to be more like Christ.

In His infinite wisdom, God teaches the strong through the weak. It isn't hearing of Shaya's great hit that brings tears to our eyes. It is the mental picture that we conjure up; 18 healthy, normal boys with torn jeans and grass-stained knees, throwing off their baseball gloves, emptying the dugout and jumping up and down. It is picturing the excitement on their dirty faces as they cheer for Shaya to run to the next base. It is the picture of a father with tears streaming down his face in joy for his son. And it is the image of a clumsy, disabled boy running to home plate, playing the part of a hero. Our hearts are touched because the story forces us to humble ourselves, and seek to be an angel to someone else.

Dear Lucas,

At some point in our lives we feel that we can change the world. Before you entered my life, I was content with my circumstances and the contributions I was making. The Lord had blessed me with a very supportive family. I was active in my church. I loved my job at the local high school where I had the opportunity to work with my best friends every day. We were "impacting the lives" of our students.

Then, your dad took the position of high school principal and in only a matter of days I met your mom, your brothers...and you. It wasn't long before your mom asked me to ride along on the first of many trips to Sioux Falls for your doctor visits, during which we also stopped at the mall to do some serious shopping!

After that first trip, your mom and I were visiting in the living room when you rolled across the floor to my feet, looked up and gave me the biggest grin I'd ever seen. From that moment on, Lucas, you've had my heart. And what made it beautiful is that you had no idea. You had nothing to gain and no ulterior motive...you were just being you! It didn't take me long to realize that you were giving me far more than I ever gave to you.

Lucas, you've taught me that it takes no words at all to love someone unconditionally. Spending time with you makes time stand still – no worries, no pretense, no need to hurry on to something else – just you and me enjoying each other's company.

You've taught me the "little" lessons, like how much happier you are when I walk beside you to guide your chair down the hallway, rather than pushing you from behind. That's what we all want!

Lucas, I've never seen someone's eyes shine quite like yours do when you're excited. And it's your excitement for the simple pleasures that has taught me to actively appreciate the simple pleasures in my own life. You've taught me to fully focus on those I'm spending time with and to tell them how much they mean to me. You've taught me to use more of my time helping and encouraging others; focusing on their unspoken needs.

My life is more beautiful today and it's all because you have changed my world!

Thank you, Lucas! I love you!

Ruth

Life...It's Either Going to
Tear You Apart or Bond You Together

I was 36 years old when I was invited to share my thoughts about serving people with disabilities at a forum in Washington, D.C. It would be my first trip to D.C. so I gladly accepted the invitation. In fact, since Darla, Hans, and Josh hadn't been there either, I decided to take them along so that our family could experience our nation's capital together.

Almost immediately upon landing in Washington, D.C. we were confronted with monuments honoring the men and women who have shaped our country's history. The faces and figures of our country's heroes are scattered abundantly throughout D.C., carved in granite and stone. They've been marbleized and memorialized.

Our family spent hours visiting such sites. We viewed the tribute to Thomas Jefferson. We viewed the tributes to Christopher Columbus, George Washington, and Abraham Lincoln. We read about their lives and the sacrifices that each one made. Everywhere we went there were reminders of heroism.

Heroes inspire us. If they didn't, we would not go to such great lengths to honor them with extravagant monuments and immortalize them in books and movies.

So what is the essence of a true hero? I believe that a hero is a common person who faces extraordinary challenges with uncommon courage, exceptional attitude, and unyielding dignity. It is a person who has chosen to rise above circumstance. When others throw their hands up in defeat, the hero presses on and stays the course.

I love to visit Washington, D.C. and celebrate our country's heroes. There is a stirring in my soul when I am confronted with the men and women who have gone before me, who have paved the way for my freedoms through intense focus and narrow purpose.

People will always be in search of heroes. In fact, I believe that the society we live in today, more than any other in our nation's history, is in search of a specific sort of hero... heroes called moms and dads. They may not be aware of it, but today's kids are longing for moms and dads to be champions of marriage; wholly committed to one another for a lifetime. They want to know that their parents are serious about the vows they took, not because the words were pretty, but because they gave their word.

The lighting of the unity candle is a beautiful picture of God's plan for marriage. Two individual flames joining to make a single flicker of light, an inseparable union symbolizing what God calls "one flesh." Marriage was designed to be between one man and one woman, living as a single entity under the headship of Christ.

Regrettably, today's society has come to see marriage as nothing more than a casual agreement. Marriage is no longer defined by oneness, but viewed as a crapshoot with 50/50 odds. Our communities are brimming with failed marriages, broken wedding vows, and moms and dads who have not stayed narrowly focused on their roles as husbands and wives.

Divorce has a sobering effect on children. The Heritage Foundation, a public policy research organization based in Washington, D.C., gave the following report:

Mounting evidence in social science journals demonstrates that the devastating physical, emotional, and financial effects that divorce is having on these children will last well into adulthood and affect future generations. Among these broad and damaging effects are the following:

- *Children whose parents have divorced are increasingly the victims of abuse. They exhibit more health, behavioral, and emotional problems, are involved more frequently in crime and drug abuse, and have higher rates of suicide.*

- *Children of divorced parents perform more poorly in reading, spelling, and math. They also are more likely to repeat a grade and to have higher dropout rates and lower rates of college graduation.*

- *Families with children that were not poor before the divorce see their income drop as much as 50 percent. Almost 50 percent of the parents with children that are going through a divorce move into poverty after the divorce.*

- *Religious worship, which has been linked to better health, longer marriages, and better family life, drops after the parents divorce.*

The divorce of parents, even if it is amiable, tears apart the fundamental unit of American society. Today, according to the Federal Reserve Board's 1995 Survey of Consumer Finance, only 42 percent of children aged 14 to 18 live in a "first marriage" family—an intact two-parent married family. It should be no surprise to find that divorce is having such profound effects on society.

On the other hand, children whose biological parents remain married are more likely to graduate from college, less likely to commit crimes, and are statistically healthier physically and emotionally. Any society is stronger when men and women uphold their commitment to marriage. The economy is stronger. The education system is stronger and people of all ages live by a higher standard of morality.

Because of the world we live in, God's perfect plan isn't always realized and divorce happens. When it does, we must pray for God's grace and protection, knowing that "He heals the brokenhearted and binds up their wounds"(Psalm 147:3). I believe that God is deeply saddened by divorce, but He loves His children and His mercies are new every morning.

Marriage is a fundamental pivot point. Civilizations, past and present, are defined by their regard for marriage. And regard for marriage is defined one household at a time.

Darla and I had a picture perfect beginning, one that is unlike many others. We were born in the same town and met in church nursery school. We went on to graduate kindergarten, elementary school, high school, and even college together.

The elementary school that Darla and I attended made a big deal about kindergarten graduation; caps, gowns, tassels, and even diplomas! On our "graduation" day, we were having our class picture taken and the teacher put me in my usual place, front row, center, where she could keep an eye on me. As I stood there waiting for the photo to be taken, very proud in my cap and gown, I glanced to my left. Right beside me stood a little girl with long dark hair, big brown eyes, and skin that was tanned to a golden brown. I thought to myself, "She's kinda cute."

She looked back at me...tall, skinny, red haired, freckle-faced, knobby knees...and thought to herself, "He's kind of a geek."

As the years passed, she got cuter and I got geekier. And I'm proud to say, that on July 30, 1983, I married that cute little girl and promised to love her for the rest of my life.

Darla and I started our married life with many things in common. We shared a community, common upbringings, and a common faith. According to research, we started out with pretty good odds for success. But there have been many times I've thought, "July 30, 1983," is a way of reflecting on our incredible ignorance as we stood at the altar over twenty years ago. We vowed to love each other for better or for worse, for richer or poorer, in sickness and in health. We said the words and we meant the words, but we didn't understand the words. We didn't have a clue how much work was ahead of us.

Life in today's world is tough and seems to be getting

tougher. Marriage in our world is tough and seems to be getting tougher. So we have a choice to make. We can complain about the difficulties or we can embrace them. We can pat ourselves on the back and walk away from a difficult marriage feeling that we did our best, but it simply wasn't meant to be. Or we can tap into the hero within us and face the difficulties in our marriage with uncommon courage, exceptional attitude, and unyielding dignity. Of course, that is easier said than done.

When Lucas was recovering from full spinal fusion surgery, there were many moments when he was fighting for his life. I remember looking at his unresponsive, little body and kissing him goodbye as they wheeled him away for a second surgery. Darla and I were completely wiped out physically and emotionally. When we sat down together in the surgical waiting room, again I uttered the words, "July 30, 1983." Moments like that, like the ones we've faced over and over with Lucas, never even entered my mind on our wedding day.

Marriage is naturally stressful. There is financial stress, the stress of raising kids, the stress of daily demands on your time and energy, and the stress of living with someone else's quirks. These are common frustrations that every family faces, but adding a child with disabilities dramatically increases the tension in a marriage.

When we were faced with the reality of parenting a disabled child, it dramatically increased the stress factor in our marriage. Although we've always been comfortable financially, the birth of Lucas created obvious financial stress, medications, fulltime medical care, frequent emergency room visits, and extended stays in intensive care.

In addition to financial pressure, our emotional stress has gone through the proverbial roof at times. We didn't anticipate parenting a child with severe disabilities, yet there he was. We've had to deal with the fear of the unknown as well as the fear of the known. Add in prolonged times of separation, when one parent is staying at the hospital with Lucas while the other is caring for the boys at home, and one would agree that our emotional wellbeing has been taxed.

We've been bombarded with the physical stress of fatigue. Many nights have been virtually void of sleep; waking to the sound of monitors, administering medications, managing seizures, or simply checking to see if he's still breathing.

The birth of Lucas has also created spiritual stress, questioning God tirelessly at times: What's the purpose? Why Lucas? Why us? At times the spiritual strain has driven us to our knees in prayer and to the scriptures for comfort. Other times it has driven us away from God, even causing us to questioning His existence. Ultimately it has deepened our faith, making us stronger through adversity, but it has often been a painful process.

When I coached basketball, my teams became very familiar with the instructions to "Focus, focus, focus." If we could just focus for eight minutes a quarter, four quarters at a time, then we would have a great chance of winning the game. Focus, focus, focus for thirty-two minutes of every game on executing the plan and employing the fundamentals.

It's no different in the "game" of marriage. Focus, focus, focus...every day, whether apart or together, executing God's plan and employing the fundamentals. We must choose to focus on living as one flesh, indivisible, with Christ as the head of our homes. Focus, focus, focus...every day...on serving one another and putting the cause above ourselves, our spouses and our children above ourselves, because a healthy marriage truly resembles a winning team.

A team is two or more people coming together to accomplish a common goal. It is safe to assume that a couple, on their wedding day, shares the common goal of loving one another for a lifetime. So what makes them give up on that goal? They lose right focus. They begin focusing on the good of the individual rather than the good of the team. It doesn't work in basketball games and it won't work in marriage. Winning teams are made up of individuals that are focused on earning the trust of their teammates and who are willing to serve one another. They value self-sacrifice and they realize that rising above obstacles will make the victories even sweeter. When a good team wins, it celebrates individual successes. When a good team loses, it shoulders the loss together, each member assessing their own contribution to the failure and never pointing fingers. Winning teams stay focused. They see the end in sight. They see the goal. And the "end" is what drives them.

A winning marriage stays focused on the goal. It is driven by the desire, the goal, to leave a positive legacy for the next generation. It refuses to focus on the good of the individual, but is determined to pursue the good of the team. It finds the strength to endure, because it dares to dream about the good that can be accomplished.

I believe we should approach our marriages like we would a basketball game. We should dream together. We should encourage one another. We should work hard together. We should believe that success is possible, even in the face of adversity. And we should remind each other often of the goal. Some of the best basketball games have been won in the final seconds, by teams who have fought from behind to take the lead. The best basketball games were never played by teams that gave up at halftime.

I believe that God clearly expects husbands to accept the role of coach, to fulfill the responsibility of creating team-work in the home. In Ephesians 5:25 it says, "Husbands, love your wives, just as Christ loved the church and gave himself up for her." Men, we are told to love our wives as Christ loves the church. Wow! Christ loved the church so much that He *died* for it. His own people, His church, spat on Him, beat Him and called Him names. They wished Him nothing but harm and yet He said, "Father, forgive them" (Luke 23:34). Do I love my wife with that kind of love? Do you love your spouse with that kind of love? God expects us to defend our wife, not condemn her. We are expected to protect her, cherish her, and present her without blemish.

Later in Ephesians it says that husbands are to love their wives as they love their own bodies. There is an enor-mous responsibility on the shoulders of men. And men must rise to the challenge if they want their marriages to succeed. If we want to leave a legacy that our children will be proud of, then we must become leaders of our households. Not in a heavy handed manor, but as servants.

I have dropped the ball many times in our marriage, using my leadership role as a thing of power rather than one of service. I married the right person, but believe that I married her when I was too young and too immature to understand the magnitude of my role as a husband. Early in our marriage, life was all about me, not about us and not at all about being the leader of a winning team. I was selfish and indulgent.

Thank God that he used Darla to grow me up and that He has blessed and protected our marriage over the years. I love Darla deeply, but I haven't always acted lovingly toward her. I've had to learn to love her and our boys sacrificially, with the heart of a servant...the heart of Christ. It's a calling that no man can ever perfect. It's a lifelong process that can be incredibly difficult some days, but one that we must embrace if we are focused on leaving a legacy of leadership and integrity.

The most heroic thing moms and dads can do is to love one another, putting cause above self. When we put our marriages above ourselves, our kids above ourselves, society above ourselves, and our country above ourselves, then we are learning to love heroically.

The Bible tells us that love bears all things, believes all things, hopes all things, and endures all things (I Corinthians 13:7). Although Lucas has brought a tremendous amount of stress into our marriage and family, his presence has also taught us the essence of true love. He has taught us the importance of pulling together as a couple in the midst of chaos and pain, and to focus, focus, focus.

Darla and I have had to focus on creating a winning team. If we would have focused on the inconvenience and stress, it would have torn our marriage apart years ago. More than twenty years later, I still reflect on the date, "July 30,

1983." We didn't have a clue. In many ways, we still don't have a clue and that's okay. It's okay that we don't know what is on our horizon because we know that we are committed to one another. We want to be in the ranks of married heroes. We want our life together to speak to the next generation, saying that for better or worse, we are one in Christ until death do us part.

Dear Lucas,

It was great to see you today. Your brothers, Ruth, and I had a great time being with you. Your mom wishes she could have joined us, but there were things at home that needed her attention.

Mom's absence made me think about your future. I don't always miss your mom when she's not with me… but today I did. For some reason it made me think of what life would be like if I weren't married. Your mom is my life partner and my best friend.

I love your mom and she loves me. Although I knew your mom was pretty the first time I saw her, today she is the most beautiful person I know.

Mom and I are fortunate. We have grown more in love with one another through our years of marriage. And I believe your life was the impetus for this growth. We didn't know where to turn after you were born so we turned to each other. Then we turned to God. It's true that when there is nowhere to run and nowhere to hide, you find God. In our case, we rediscovered each other in the process of seeking Him.

You are not likely to experience marriage, but your life makes our marriage better. You will not have children of your own, but your life has a positive impact on parents. You will not run, jump, or play like others, but you inspire athletes and those of us who are "normal" to maximize our potential and give thanks for our abilities.

Your future will certainly look different than that of other boys your age, but your life provides unique perspective and motivation that will make the futures of others more dynamic.

God has used your life to help me fall deeper in love with your mom. Along with uncertainty and complexity, your life brings us abundant love and joy. You have drawn us closer to God and closer to one another.

I'm sorry that you will never experience a first date, or prom night, or the love of a spouse, but take heart in knowing that your life has multiplied our love and made our marriage, and our family, more beautiful. I love you, kid.

Leadership Isn't Optional

Sitting in the office of one of my mentors, a man who spent many years as an educator and then as the Chief Executive Officer of an organization serving people with disabilities, I inquired how I might better understand Lucas, how I could be a more effective father to Lucas, and how Darla and I could be certain that we were doing everything possible to give Lucas the best quality of life.

After listening patiently to my concerns about parenting a disabled son, my friend responded with a message I hadn't anticipated, but one that I will never forget. Although my questions were all about Lucas, his answers were not. Instead, he addressed the parental responsibility that Darla and I have to our "normal" children. I was intrigued as he talked with me about a common pitfall of parents in our situation.

He explained that when a child with disabilities enters a family, the focus tends to shift entirely to the needs of that child, leaving siblings feeling slighted. The healthy children often get lost in the shuffle of daily demands, with their needs gradually taking a back seat to those of their disabled sibling. The message my friend delivered that day was simply this, *as you focus on loving Lucas and serving his needs, do not overlook the needs of your other children.* He was challenging Darla and me to be intentional in the way we parent each of our boys, not just Lucas.

When calling ambulances, coordinating medical treatments, and simply adjusting to the emotion of caring for a child with disabilities, it's very easy for time and energy to be consumed. During Lucas' first six years, there were many times that our family was divided. Darla would stay at home with Lucas while I took Hans and Josh to a ball game. I would stay home with Lucas while Darla took the rest of the family to church. We would often attend family gatherings separately so that one of us could stay home to care for Lucas. It was becoming a way of life and the advice of our friend caused us to examine the parental attitudes and actions we were developing.

It was this examination that was largely responsible for our decision to transition Lucas from our home to the full time care of CCHS. The specialized care that Lucas required had grown beyond our expertise and we believed that settling him into a specialized care facility was the right decision for him. We also believed, however, that moving Lucas was the right decision for Hans, Josh, and Logan.

Not only were we able to spend more unified time as a family, we began taking weekly family trips to visit Lucas. At least once a week we all piled into the family Suburban and drove an hour and a half to spend the day with Lucas. These have become treasured moments, with little interruption or outside interference, and God has used them to bring our family closer together.

As I have pondered the message of my mentor over the years, I've come to the conclusion that the essence of our success as parents doesn't lie within proven methods, but simply within our determination to leave something of value behind. Success is found when we are intentional about the way we approach every moment of our lives.

LEADERSHIP ISN'T OPTIONAL

Deuteronomy 6:4-9 says, "Love the Lord your God with all your heart and with all your soul and with all your strength. These commandments that I give you today are to be upon your hearts. Impress them on your children. Talk about them when you sit at home and when you walk along the road, when you lie down and when you get up. Tie them as symbols on your hands and bind them on your foreheads. Write them on the doorframes of your houses and on your gates."

First things first, love the Lord your God. Then, talk about Him in the ordinary moments...all the time. When you sit at the dining room table or drive in the car. When you go to bed at night or when you're getting ready in the morning. Every day, every moment, let your kids see that you love the Lord with all your heart, soul, and strength. Let them see it in the words you speak and the decisions you make.

We've spent many hours visiting with Hans, Josh, and Logan about the journey of Lucas. We've talked openly about the decision and struggle of moving Lucas to a fulltime facility. We've talked with them about the fact that they may be responsible to care for their brother someday, if Darla and I are gone. We've talked to them about loving Lucas as a member of our family even though he doesn't live in our home.

Not only have our boys grown to love Lucas deeply, they have developed a love and concern for others with special needs. For Darla and me, the best part about parent-teacher conferences isn't the academic report, but the compassion report. It gives us great joy to hear that our children are quick to reach out to their classmates who are being teased or who need a helping hand. And I believe that they have learned to be compassionate because they've seen others show compassion for Lucas.

They've learned that Lucas is valuable to our family simply because he is their brother, not because of what he looks like or what he has to offer. When we take Lucas to a public event, such as a basketball game, our kids are never embarrassed by him. Lucas has helped us to leave a legacy of compassion, teaching our boys to love the unlovely and to serve those with special needs as Christ did.

Every situation in our day is a tool, a legacy-building tool. We can take advantage of ordinary moments, grabbing hold of them to show our children how to live a life of integrity, or we can simply get through the day. Each of us has a choice. We can leave a legacy of excellence or of mediocrity.

My dad lost his parents in a car accident when he was thirteen years old. He was the oldest child in the family and it was a time in history when he was required to fend for himself. It would have been easy for him to be angry with God and resent his circumstances, but he didn't. He chose to focus on making something of himself and seeking God's purpose for his life.

My parents have had to bury three of their children: an infant, a six-year-old, and a young adult. Despite incredible heartache, my parents often talk of being grateful for the time that they had, thankful that God entrusted them with these children even though their time on earth was short. Of course we saw our parents grieve. They have experienced a range of emotion over the years, but they have continually verbalized an attitude of acceptance of God's timing and His sovereignty.

The lessons I learned simply by watching and listening to my parents react to the situations in their lives have been invaluable. Whether extraordinary moments or ordinary ones, my parents have taught me the importance of turning to God when dealing with difficult circumstances.

True colors are displayed in the midst of adversity. How do you respond when things don't go your way? It is in these moments that we are shaping the next generation. I believe that the verses in Deuteronomy are teaching us how to leave an excellent legacy. They teach us to be intentional in talking with our kids about the everyday stuff of life. The things that are passed from generation to generation are the things that are rehearsed in our homes on good days and difficult days, and we leave a positive legacy when our daily habits reflect that we love the Lord with all our heart, soul, and strength.

Ronald Reagan is one of my heroes. Obviously, he left our country a great legacy through his service as Governor of California and then as President. He inspired many through the way he lived and the passion with which he spoke, but none were so touched by his life than his own children.

It was heartwarming, the day of Ronald Reagan's funeral, to hear his children give their tributes to their dad; not Governor Reagan, not President Reagan...just Dad. They talked about how he prepared them for his death, assuring them that he would be in Heaven because he knew Jesus Christ as his Savior. They talked about the way his life reflected the love he had for God.

When his daughter, Patty, gave her eulogy[7] she told a precious story of how her father used an ordinary moment to teach a valuable life lesson. This was her reflection:

[My dad] was the one who generously offered funeral services for my goldfish on the morning of its demise. We went out into the garden and we dug a tiny grave with a teaspoon and he took two twigs and lashed them together with twine and formed a cross as a marker for the grave. And then he gave a beautiful eulogy.

He told me that my fish was swimming in the clear blue waters in heaven and he would never tire and he would never get hungry and he would never be in any danger and he could swim as far and wide as he wanted and he never had to stop, because the river went on forever. He was free. When we went back inside and I looked at my remaining goldfish in their aquarium with their pink plastic castle and their colored rocks, I suggested that perhaps we should kill the others so they could also go to that clear blue river and be free.

He then took more time out of his morning —I'm sure he actually did have other things to do that day—and patiently explained to me that in God's time, the other fish would go there, as well. In God's time, we would all be taken home. And even though it sometimes seemed a mystery, we were just asked to trust that God's time was right and wise.

What a powerful legacy Ronald Reagan left for his daughter; a legacy that doesn't fear death but embraces the idea of eternity with anticipation. Through the death of a goldfish, he taught her that all life has value, that Heaven is a place of beauty, and that God's timing is perfect even when it doesn't make sense. If he would have simply flushed the dead goldfish, he would have robbed his daughter of a treasured lesson; one that gave her great comfort at the time of his own death and one that will surely be passed on to the next generation.

When Hans was seventeen years old, the two of us attended a men's conference together. Much of the information we were given that weekend wasn't new to us. In fact, it wasn't the information that challenged me. It was knowing that my teenage son was a witness to the information that I was receiving. I knew that he would be watching me as we returned home to see if my life would reflect the principles that were taught at the conference. Whether he knew it or not, he would be taking notes: Is my dad truly a Promise Keeper? When things don't go his way, does my dad still follow God's principles?

In our fast-paced, professional world people often say "It's not what you know, it's who you know." Although I understand the concept, I believe it goes one step further. It's not *what* you know and it's not *who* you know, but it's *what you know* about *who you know*. We are hungry for authenticity. We want people's actions to reflect their words. In reality, our names, titles, and bank accounts are far less meaningful than the way we live our daily lives.

In 2 Corinthians 3:1-3, Paul writes, "Are we beginning to commend ourselves again? Or do we need, like some people, letters of recommendation to you or from you? You yourselves are our letter, written on our hearts, known and read by everybody....written not with ink but with the Spirit of the living God, not on tablets of stone but on tablets of human hearts."

Paul tells us to cut to the chase. It doesn't matter what we say about ourselves. It doesn't matter what others say about us. It doesn't matter how many votes we get or what is written in our resumes. The only thing that matters is what people learn when they read the letters of our lives. What do they see? What's important? What isn't?

Mom, you are a letter. Dad, you are a letter. Teacher, boss, grandparent, high school student...each of you is a letter. Your life is read by the world. Does it say that you love God with all your heart, soul, and strength? Does it say that your words match your actions or does it say that you're a hypocrite?

There are days when I don't want people to read my letter. I'd rather not be proofed by the world. But most days, viewing my life as a letter gives me great energy and inspiration. If my life is an open book, then I want to keep my focus where the focus needs to be. I want to be intentional about leaving a legacy.

When Lucas was at the University of Iowa Hospital, I had the opportunity to visualize the passing on of a legacy. Lucas had gone into a severe state of distress. Darla and I were in his hospital room as it filled with medical staff. Nurses were shouting out orders and machines were shouting out warning signals. We began encouraging the doctors and nurses, talking to Lucas, and praying that God would spare the life of our son.

As I took hold of Lucas' hand, I glanced toward the doorway. There they stood, in staircase formation, just outside the hospital room. Hans, Josh, and Logan were staring intensely into the room of their brother, looking like his guardian angels. They had all seen Lucas in crisis situations before, but this time I was keenly aware that they were watching me, and watching Darla. They were observing our words, our attitudes, our actions and they were taking mental notes. I remember thinking to myself, "What message are we sending? What legacy are we leaving?" It was a picture of *generation to generation*. I knew that those moments would stay with them for the rest of their lives, and likely be passed on to their children.

Over the years, I have mastered the art of multi-tasking while driving. When I'm driving with a cup of coffee in my hand and the cell phone rings, I pick up the phone with my "free" hand, put it to my mouth, pull the antennae up with my teeth, flip the phone open with my fingers, and punch the answer button with my thumb...never taking my eyes off the road or letting go of my coffee mug. It's a habit. I do it without even thinking about the process.

One Saturday, when Josh and I were on our way home from a basketball practice, my phone rang. Instead of picking up the phone myself, I asked Josh to answer it. He had both hands free but without hesitation he picked up the phone with one hand, put it up to his mouth, pulled the antennae up with his teeth, flipped it open with his fingers, and punched the answer button with his thumb. I was speechless.

Most of the time it isn't so visible, but every now and

then God gives us a glimpse of the legacy we're leaving. When I saw my children standing in staircase formation, watching me from the hospital hallway, it was a snapshot of how closely my children observe me in the extraordinary moments. When I saw Josh answer my phone, exactly as I do, it was a snapshot of how closely my children observe me in the ordinary moments. Every moment, simple or grand, our kids are looking and watching. What are they seeing?

When Logan sees me putting on a tie, he frequently asks, "Who you speaking to tonight, Dad?" It's as if he is saying, "I know who you are, Dad. I know what you love to do. I'm watching you. And I'm learning."

Someday, on my deathbed, I hope to say, "I have fought the good fight, I have finished the race, I have kept the faith. Now there is in store for me the crown of righteousness, which the Lord, the righteous Judge, will award to me on that day..." (2 Timothy 4:6-8). More importantly, though, I hope that my boys will be able to say that about me.

I hope that the ordinary moments that I've shared with them have taught them to live lives of integrity, passion, and faith. I hope that I will have handled the extraordinary moments in such a way that inspires them to be men of character. And, most of all, I hope that they will find great comfort in knowing that I am in Heaven, in the presence of the Holy God, not because of my performance on earth, but because I believed in Christ's sacrifice for my sin.

When I tuck Logan into bed at night, I say, "I love you, Logan."

He says, "I love you, too, Dad."
"I like you, Logan."
"I like you, too, Dad."
"You're the best, Logan."
"Nah, we're both the best, Dad."

The success of our lives is ultimately determined by the legacy we leave behind. Eighteenth century author, Johann von Schiller[8], wrote, "He who has done his best for his own time has lived for all times." Each of us has the privilege and responsibility of impacting those to come after us. We must choose, in ordinary moments and extraordinary ones, to be intentional about leaving a legacy of excellence for the next generation.

A LETTER TO LUCAS,
FROM OUR OLDEST SON, HANS:

Dear Lucas,

When people ask who has been the most influential person in my life, I never have to stop and think. Without a doubt, you are the one who has crafted the way I view my life and the lives of others. After hearing my answer, those same people usually ask how a person who cannot talk can have such significant influence or teach in any way. Well, quite frankly, those people don't know you. I think that every person who has met you has been changed because of you.

I have often wondered why God made you the way you are. I've had feelings of sadness and anger, but mostly just confusion. I couldn't find any reason why you were created with such severe disabilities when the Bible says that everyone is made perfectly. For the longest time, I couldn't find God's perfection in you and it gave me doubts. Being a teenager, I know all about doubts. When you're younger, everything is black and white and easy but as you grow older, a lot of things turn gray. Things that used to seem clear begin to turn upside down in your mind and you find yourself wondering about them.

In my case, I began to wonder whether or not God is real. I never told Mom or Dad this, but that question stayed on my mind for a long time. I'd gone to church with our family since I was a baby and had been told by every significant person in my life that God is real, as if it was something that required no thought. I could see this beautifully created world, with God's fingerprints all over it. Yet, I could also see the terrible things in this world and I just had so many questions: Why was Lucas created this way? Why did my friend, Archie, have to get in that accident and become paralyzed? If there are so many abortions and so many unwanted babies in this world, why doesn't God give babies to desiring couples who would make awesome parents? On a more of a global scale, why is there always war? Why do innocent kids die of disease and starvation all over the world?

Well, Lucas, I know I'll never have the answers to all my questions, but because of you, I don't have to.

What I used to see as imperfection in you now looks like perfection. You are the example. You live the way we are all supposed to live.

You have it worse than any other person I know, yet you smile more than any person I know. You can't do any of the things that "normal" people can do, but you never feel sorry for yourself. To be honest, you amaze me. If I suddenly found myself in your condition, I wouldn't even want to live, but you're the happiest person I know. You go into a violent seizure and come out of it laughing. I don't get it.

My own "huge problems" are nothing compared to yours, but I still get downhearted more often than you. I get stressed over a fight with a girl, while you come out of near-death experiences unfazed. Once again, I don't get it.

You change me every time I see you, Lucas. For all these reasons, you continue to influence me and make me better.

More than anything, I feel God's presence when I'm with you. I can't really explain it, I just know. You may not be able to talk, but you are a great witness. You make me realize that God has a purpose for everything even though we may never understand it, and it's okay if we don't because He is God and we are not.

Thanks for everything, Lucas. I love you.

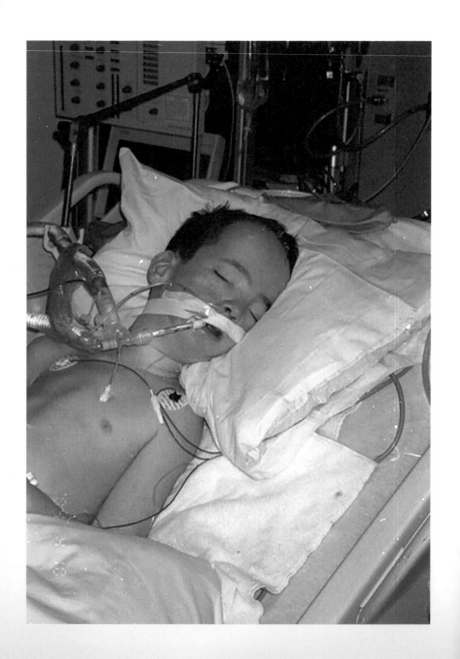

It's Not for Us to Understand

Our society thrives on change; the newest, most improved, and never-seen-anything-like-it-before. We are conditioned to find ways to better our homes, our bodies, our intellects, and our careers. We enjoy change, but we want it on our terms. We want the fairytale. We want control. In fact, in our self-driven world we have become writers of our own destinies; confident in our own abilities to determine and deliver what is best. We accept change when it feels good. But when change is unexpected or painful, when we hit a bump in the road - or a crater - it often leaves us feeling insecure; full of questions, frustration, and stress.

In January of 1996, Darla and I were living in Sheldon with our three young boys, where I was the Sheldon High School principal. Our life there was familiar and secure. We were very content with our circumstances, not looking for a change, when I received an offer to become the CEO of Opportunities Unlimited (OU) in Sioux City; a non-profit organization serving people with disabilities. Not only would this mean a change in career path, but also the need to relocate our family. The proverbial pros and cons list was well in favor of staying in Sheldon. There were so many reasons to stay and so few reasons to go, but we couldn't deny the prompting we felt to go for it; to leave behind the comfort and security that we knew, and move to Sioux City.

The potential of OU's mission inspired me, yet the

organization was on a fast downward spiral as it was issued fifty-four pages of state deficiencies - not fifty-four items - fifty-four *pages*. It was in need of a corporate CPR.

I love a challenge, so I rolled up my sleeves, determined to deliver a success story. It wasn't long before the reality of the situation set in. While we were making progress clinically, we were definitely day-to-day financially. Less than six weeks after taking the helm, a board member advised me to keep my career options open, signaling the corporation's on going concern. In addition to the clinical and financial hurdles that needed to be cleared, the office building was in a less-than-desirable location, making safety a concern. And in an on going effort to implement a culture committed to fulfilling OU's mission with excellence, I made daily determinations of who would stay on the team and who would be made available for employment elsewhere. These decisions were not easy as I knew they had life-altering implications.

Any job change creates stress, but I gave up a job with a dependable paycheck and government funding in exchange for a 60-minute commute (one way), to work for an organization that may or may not survive the week. Major stress!

Darla and I began to scout the real estate listings for a house in Sioux City and to prepare our home in Sheldon for sale. Relocating a family of five is no simple task. We eventually decided to purchase two acres of land tucked into the beautiful rolling hills of Sioux City's northeast side, and to build a new house. Afterall, we were not going to have any more children so we were ready to spend some money and brain power creating the perfect home for our family, complete with all the amenities necessary for accommodating the special needs of Lucas.

Pouring myself into the restoration of OU was an inspiring challenge, demanding an incredible measure of mental and emotional energy. In addition, our three boys still needed their dad to be fully engaged. We were continually adjusting to Lucas' disabilities, trying to keep up with Hans' and Josh's activities, and making the many arrangements and decisions that come with building a new home. My life was full. Or at least I *thought* it was, until Darla called me at the office one day to announce that she was pregnant! I remember asking God, "Why? I left a job and community I loved because You prompted me to do it, and You decide to reward me with a pregnant wife?" Major stress!

Eight months later our little white tornado was born, whom we named Logan and my parents have affectionately coined as 'payback'. Logan was such an unexpected blessing and his arrival brought a great deal of healing to our family. He was the little brother that Hans and Josh could play with, and he completed things for Lucas too, giving him brothers in front and behind. Only God knew what we really needed and what we were capable of handling. Isaiah 55:9 says, "As the Heavens are higher than the earth, so are my ways higher than your ways and my thoughts than your thoughts." In my limited, human understanding I thought that another child would simply be a burden...one more thing consuming my time and money. In God's abundant wisdom, He knew that Logan would not be a burden at all, but would bring the kind of joy and vitality that I didn't even realize I needed.

During that season of life, we were forced to embrace change over and over again. Some of it was by our own choosing and some was not. Some of it was frightening and some of it exhilarating, but God used each situation to show me, in a very tangible way, that He is in control and He knows what is best.

Fast forward to April 30, 2004. Lucas was now ten years old and had been in the hospital, in and out of intensive care, for nearly a month following spinal fusion surgery. Because the hospital was seventy-five miles from our home, Darla stayed with Lucas while I stayed in Sioux City to care for Hans, Josh and Logan. Darla's tireless devotion during those difficult days was a tribute to motherhood. She wanted to stay with Lucas, but we both knew that she needed a break and arranged to switch roles for a couple of days.

My first day at the hospital was a good one. Lucas was doing well and I enjoyed being by his side, kissing his head and singing his favorite songs. That evening I made my bed on the pullout couch in his room, and finally fell asleep shortly after midnight, just in time to be awakened by his cries. Thinking that he simply needed to be changed or repositioned, I ventured into the brightly lit hospital hallway to ask for assistance.

Moments later, two nurses began working with Lucas to determine what was making him uncomfortable, quickly discovering that his IV line had blown. They informed me that a new line would have to be started. This was disappointing news in view of the fact that he had extremely small veins, turning a simple procedure into a tedious and painful event. As the flight technician, who was called in to start the IV, began the process, I tried to help by holding Lucas' head in my hands, distracting him from the repeated pricks and pokes to his arm and keeping his eyes fixed on me. As they continued working on him, he became totally silent - too silent. I looked at his chest. It wasn't moving. I studied his face. He wasn't breathing. I felt his skin. It was burning up.

In the midst of a sudden outbreak of activity, I backed away as they ceased their efforts with the IV, put a breathing bag over his nose and mouth, and began to resuscitate him. Once he was breathing again they took his temperature. 105.7 degrees. Before I could process the situation they were rushing him to the Intensive Care Unit, still trying to start the IV.

Do I call Darla? The question was repeating in my mind, when one of the nurses instructed me to do so. It was the middle of the night. She would have to drive ninety minutes, all alone, to get to the hospital. And I knew the nurse was right...I had to call. Darla was already awake when the phone rang, feeling she should be in Sioux Falls with Lucas. When she arrived at the hospital, she described her drive as emotional, using the miles to have a very passionate, honest discussion with God while yelling her frustration through tears.

Lucas' tiny veins kept collapsing, making it nearly impossible to start the IV that was so vitally needed. He was enveloped in cooling blankets, but his temperature kept rising. Finally, just before Darla arrived, they were able to access one of the carotids and get him stabilized. At 4 a.m. I found a spot to lie down and was able to sleep until Darla woke me a few hours later telling me that his temperature had climbed to 106.9 degrees. Again, I went to his side, held his head in my hands, and talked to him. We had been through many critical situations with Lucas, but it never became easy. It was so difficult to see him connected to machines, with cords coming and going from his body, looking so lifeless. Moments later, he began having a major seizure and I thought, "This is it."

Despite my fears, the medical team was able to get him stabilized once again. Our nerves were running thin and emotions running high when we received a much needed answer to prayer. An entire surgical team appeared outside Lucas' door, as if from nowhere, on a Saturday morning. There was the surgeon, with gown on, his assistant, and all the professionals needed to make, and carry out, the decision to reopen and irrigate Lucas' incision flushing out the staph infection that had taken up residence in his back.

Darla and I started down the hallway with Lucas and the medical team, accompanying them to the operating room. As we stood in the elevator, the intensive care nurse began reporting Lucas' vital statistics to the surgical nurse. When she reported his temperature to be 107 degrees, the surgical nurse must have forgotten that we were present, and said, "Oh my God!" It sent a chill down my spine, and again I thought, "This is it."

As we sat in the waiting room, Darla and I began to plan a funeral, yet prayed that God would allow him to survive the surgery. God answered that prayer, and Lucas began a very slow and rocky recovery.

As parents, we instinctively fought for the life of our child, yet there were moments in that waiting room when, in my human understanding, it made sense for God to take Lucas while he was under anesthetic, without pain or fear. In Heaven his disabilities will be fully restored allowing him to run, and sing, and play. It made sense to me that streets of pure gold and seas of crystal will be far better for him than ICU hallways and IV needles. God's ways are higher than our ways, His thoughts higher than our thoughts and He always knows what is best, even when we don't understand.

When I returned to work on Monday I was met with irony. I learned that a woman in our community had been jogging when she was hit and killed by a pick-up truck. She and her husband had been deeply in love, with a marriage that inspired other couples. She was a stay-at-home mom, happily devoted to their four young children. The questions were relentless; why would God allow this beloved wife and mother to be killed, yet sustain the life of Lucas? Why are old men and women lying in nursing homes, wishing to die, and yet they live? Lucas touched death many times, reaching out his hand as if to say, "Here I am, God," yet his life was spared.

Why? Because God's thoughts are higher than our thoughts, His ways are higher than our ways, and it's not for us to understand.

Even Jesus grieved. He grieved at the thought of His own death (Luke 22:42-44) and He grieved the death of His friend (John 11:33-36). Surely Jesus had an intimate understanding of the mind of His Heavenly Father, yet He still experienced sorrow and pain. People often say that they have a list of questions to ask God when they get to Heaven, but when we actually get there and see Him face to face - when we see the whole of His plan in place - maybe we will simply say, "Of course, now it all makes sense." When we are in His presence, able to focus on Him, our questions may become suddenly insignificant.

When we took our boys to visit my sister in Michigan, she took us to the local mall, which had a massive rock climbing wall. Being Dutch, I don't part with money easily, but we were on vacation and I was feeling generous, so I told the boys that we would pay for them to climb the wall. Logan, our little white tornado, was the only one to accept the challenge. He was six years old and fearless. He had been observing as teenagers and adults, attempting to reach the top, lost their grip and fell away from the wall at the same protruding point. But he was ready to go!

As they were strapping on his harness, he looked up at me and asked if I was planning to climb with him. "Uh-huh. I'm not climbing any wall," I said, "but I'll be right here to encourage you and talk you through it." A few moments later he was on his way up and I was cheering him on. "Hey, good job, Logan! Push off with your left foot. Now reach up with your right hand. Grab on. Hold on tight."

Our family's cameras were working overtime, and to my surprise, Logan was doing pretty well. As he reached the section of the wall that had defeated most adults, he grabbed on tight, trying to move to safety, but suddenly let go. The belt around his small body suspended him far above our heads, inches from the wall. I thought, "Oh well, it was a good attempt, but that's it." What impressed me is that Logan never looked away. He never looked down. He just stared at the wall, reached for it, and persisted climbing. I stood there, looking up at him, thinking, "You stud!"

He continued climbing until he reached the top giving it a slap of victory, and I started yelling, "That's my son!" As we waited for them to remove his harness, we began to discuss his accomplishment. Why could Logan, a scrawny six-year-old, conquer the wall when teenagers and adults were unable to do so? Darla assessed it beautifully saying, "Because he has incredible focus when he chooses to apply it."

We are all climbing, every day, through this rocky journey called life. We encounter obstacles along the way that require us to change course, experiencing pain and fear, confusion and stress. Because life's journey is full of detours and situations that are difficult to understand, we must *choose* to focus on that which can be understood. During these stressful times our minds may not be able to comprehend the *why*, but we *can* find peace in embracing the sovereignty of God, believing that His grace is boundless and His wisdom is supreme.

God knows that we are incapable of perfection, that our struggle with sin will never be over until we leave this earth, but "...because of his great love for us, God, who is rich in mercy, made us alive with Christ even when we were dead in sin...For it is by grace that you have been saved, through faith – and this not of yourselves, it is the gift of God" (Ephesians

2:4-5, 8). What a wonderful truth! No matter how inconvenient or traumatic our situation, God loves us and sent his Son to save us from the eternal damnation we deserve. If the rest of our earthly existence was plagued with pain, the gift of His saving grace should be enough reason to press on with joy in our hearts.

Not only can we focus on God's grace, but His mighty power. For Joshua, God stopped the sun "...in the middle of the sky and delayed its going down about a full day" (Joshua 10:13-14). For the Israelites, He divided the waters of the Red Sea so they were able to pass through "...on dry ground, with a wall of water on their right and on their left" (Exodus 14: 21-22). For you and me, He overcame the power of death, raising Jesus from the dead" ...freeing him from the agony of death, because it was impossible for death to keep its hold on him" (Acts 2:24).

When we stop to ponder the wonder of His power we must also recognize His ability to fix our problems in the blink of an eye. So if He is able to shield us from pain, from the heartache of loss and the stress of uncertainty, then why does He allow us to suffer? He allows us times of suffering because in His omnipotence, He knows more than we know and sees more than we see. God promises to work the details of our lives together for good (Romans 8:28), even when it makes no sense to us. He "rained down bread from heaven" when His children were hungry (Exodus 16:4) and made drinking water come out of a rock to quench their thirst (Exodus 17:6). We must choose to focus on the fact that He *is able*, if it is for our good.

We must trust His supreme wisdom. God has an incomprehensible knowledge of the past, present, and future and an intimate knowledge of your life and mine. It's as though we are only capable of one-dimensional, black and white judgments, but His decisions are made in 3-D and full-color.

When a two-year-old tries to touch a hot stove, his parent will certainly intervene, instructing the child that the burner is hot and will burn him if he persists. The child remains intrigued, unconvinced of the danger, and continues reaching. The parent continues to act in the best interest of the child, abruptly pulling him away from the danger, and the child is left feeling deprived and unfulfilled even though he should be feeling grateful and relieved. This scenario is simple, producing little argument, but isn't this duplicated in our adult lives when we experience circumstances that leave us feeling deprived, unfulfilled, and even unloved? Sometimes we must simply trust God's wisdom above our own.

Whatever we focus on fervently is the thing that will rule us. When we choose to focus on our problems we wind up frustrated and depressed. When we focus on our own ability to control our circumstances we are left feeling worried and helpless. When we focus on that which we wish we had, we are consumed by feelings of deprivation. What would happen if we decided today to fervently focus on God and His Word? What would happen if we forced ourselves to view our problems and insufficiencies through a divine filter and to surrender our need for control?

From the first moment Lucas entered the world, it was

painfully evident that Darla and I were powerless to 'fix' him. His life journey has caused us a gamut of emotion and has taught us to pray, "Thy will be done."

Jesus didn't enjoy suffering. He didn't enjoy being spat upon, or whipped, or nailed to a cross. He didn't want to experience the pain that He knew was looming so He prayed, "My Father, if it is possible, may this cup be taken from me" (Matthew 26:39a). But He chose to trust and focus on God's wisdom rather than His own comfort. Because He chose to focus on the incredible love in His heart for you and me, He was able to pray, "If it is not possible for this cup to be taken away unless I drink it, *may your will be done*" (Matthew 26:39b). He trusted His Father's heart, even when His circumstances were frightening and uncomfortable.

We would not have chosen a son with disabilities. We never wanted to spend endless nights in the intensive care unit, holding the head of our child as he fought to take another breath. But it has been a crash course in embracing God's sovereignty. When we focus on Lucas' disabilities and deficiencies, it leaves us feeling angry and afraid, but when we focus on God's grace, power, and wisdom we find the strength to earnestly thank God for the opportunity to know Lucas, just as he is - to hold him and to love him. The quality of our lives, in response to Lucas, has depended on our focus. We have learned to trust God even when we don't understand, and to apply the words of this simple chorus:

Turn your eyes upon Jesus,
Look full in His wonderful face,
And the things of earth will grow strangely dim,
In the light of His glory and grace.

There is so much I don't understand:

I don't understand why women have to suffer during childbirth, while men simply watch.

I don't understand why so many athletes with natural, God-given abilities have such low ambition.

I don't understand why some couples are blessed with many children, while others remain barren.

I don't understand why some children are abused by their own parents.

I don't understand why some people are so abundantly blessed, while others are in a constant state of struggle.

I don't understand why you and I get to live in America, while others suffer in third-world countries.

I don't understand why people who want to die... live, and people who want to live...die.

I don't understand why you have to go through

pain and disappointments when, in my opinion, you do nothing to warrant the suffering.

I don't understand how eternity in Heaven can be a gift...free of charge.

There is much your dad doesn't understand. But I believe the reason I don't understand these things is because God never intended for us to understand the complexities of life. He simply wants me, and you, to have complete faith. All we need to understand is that He is a sovereign God who loves us enough to weave all things, pleasant and unpleasant, together for our good.

Thankfully, there is one thing that I understand perfectly. I understand that you have captured my heart.

Your life has impacted mine immeasurably and my life would not be complete without you. I carry you and your life's message with me everywhere I go.

One day our Sovereign Father and Friend will allow us to grasp His reasoning. Until then, we must trust Him. He is filled with love for you and me and He uses the things we don't understand to bring us closer to Him.

God loves you, Lucas, and so do I.

Teaching Without Ever Saying a Word

It was Monday morning. I moved quickly down the stairs and into the kitchen where I would eat breakfast with my parents. On this spring day of my senior year of high school, our basketball team would face its chief rival in the district semi-finals.

We anticipated a difficult game and my mother was well aware of my competitive nature. As I loaded my duffle bag and headed toward the back door, she stopped me and said, "I want you to know something. I want you to know that tonight you will win. Your team is going to win." I liked this positive attitude, especially from someone who had never played the game of basketball. She exuded confidence that we would defeat one of our toughest competitors despite their talent and season of success. She even reiterated the declaration in order to get her point across. In view of the fact that she knew so little about team records and game strategies, this assurance intrigued me so I asked why she was so sure that we would have victory.

Without hesitation she replied, "Bob, it's plain and simple. Your opponent practiced on the Sabbath and God will not honor the abuse of His Holy Day. Their team practiced on the Sabbath, so they will lose. Your team didn't, so you will win." Simple. No gray area. No doubt. And the irony was that I believed it completely. As I walked out the door and headed to school, it never occurred to me to question her theory.

You see, my family, church, and school all taught me the

same thing about this cause and effect relationship regarding good deeds and bad deeds. The lesson was clear that God rewards those who keep His commandments and punishes those who don't. Afterall, the Old Testament is full of examples. Chapter twenty-six of Leviticus says, "If you follow my decrees and are careful to obey my commands, I will send rain in season. But if you will not listen to me and carry out all these commands, then I will do this to you, I will bring upon you sudden terror, wasting disease and fever." These words are uncomplicated with little room for misinterpretation. Simple. No gray area. No doubt. Just like Mom.

When Old Testament passages like this merged with an upbringing that reinforced the concept, it's no wonder that the arrival of Lucas caused me to look within. Questions immediately flooded my mind. What did I do? Why is God choosing to punish me through a son who isn't right?

Despite many questions, there was one certainty. If God was choosing to use Lucas as some sort of reprimand, then it was definitely meant for me. Not Darla. If you were to study the life of Darla, you would quickly discover that she was deserving of sainthood simply for putting up with me. No, this reproof was not for her. It must have been for me and the result was a serious look in the mirror. What exactly was I being punished for?

As I began to survey my life, one thing became evident. I talked a great talk, but my walk had been very weak. I talked enthusiastically about priorities: God first, then family, then country. It sounded good. It looked good. But a closer look revealed a contradiction. I talked of these priorities, but my walk proved that the pursuit of success received much more energy and attention than God or my family. At the end of the day, winning basketball games was what mattered. Period. I was far more in sync with career advancement than the advancement of God's kingdom or the development of my family.

My life was fast-paced and full-throttle. College was followed by a good teaching job and a head coaching position. At twenty-nine I became a high school principal, despite being one of the youngest staff members at that school. Everything was in gear and life was moving along exactly as planned. So what was the problem? Life had become all about me and not about God.

The conclusion of this life assessment was this: If God had a Leviticus moment and saw the need to send me a message, then the message was clear and the messenger was a son named Lucas. The biggest question that remained was "Why him?" If I was the one that needed a reality check, why not inflict the harm on me - on my body? Let *me* suffer ill health. Let *me* experience the pain of countless needles and a lifetime of dependence on others.

Why not me? Because God knew that I prided myself in being an incredibly strong person, determined to rise above the difficult circumstances of life. He knew that it would take more than the usual 2x4 to get my attention.

God has an intimate knowledge of His children, and is fully aware of the exact circumstance that will bring us to complete reliance on Him. He knew that Lucas was the very "thing" that would bring me to my knees quickly. I was completely helpless. I couldn't change a thing. I couldn't make him right, and the guilt was relentless. Was Lucas meant to be a punishment for my poor choices? If I had been more responsible or more spiritual, would he have been born healthy?

Jesus himself responded to a similar question in John 9:1-3, and His answer has given me great solace. When Jesus and His followers happen upon a blind man, they approach him and the disciples ask, "Who sinned, this man or his parents, that he was born blind?" Afterall, the disciples had received the very same Old Testament teaching that I had, infirmity is the result of bad behavior.

At this point I imagine that Jesus might have simply smiled, knowing that they just didn't get it. He answers them gently, "No one sinned. This occurred so that the work of God might be displayed in his life." The reason that this man was born with a disability was so that the work of God might be displayed in his life. Reflecting on this story has helped me to sincerely thank God for Lucas.

It gives me great comfort to say, "No one sinned." When Jesus made that statement he was not declaring that the man or his parents were sinless. Rather, he was affirming that human inadequacies are purposeful and the challenges of life are not necessarily the result of our sin. Rather, our challenges and infirmities offer opportunities for God to reveal His mercy and grace. He knows full well that we *all have sinned and fall short of his glory* (Romans 3:23).

Before Lucas was born, God knew every sin I ever committed, every bad choice I ever made, and yet He forgave me. He knows your every sin, and yet He chose to die. His love for me, for Lucas, and for you is so great that *while we were still sinners he died for us* (Romans 5:8). There is great freedom in acknowledging our imperfections, and great power in embracing the cross.

With a few words, thousands of years ago, Jesus revealed the purpose for Lucas' life. Our son was not brought into this world as a punishment for anyone's sin, but to be a reflection of God's wonder, an instrument of God's mercy, and a catalyst to make me more like Christ. Through his human frailty, Lucas has inspired the competent and challenged the strong.

A close family friend once described how Lucas has been used in her life to reveal the character of God:

> *He is full of joy, peace, patience (most of the time), kindness, goodness, gentleness, and he exudes unconditional love. He isn't impressed with a person's worldly status, doesn't care much about receiving things, and isn't mindful of what others think of him. He just loves for me to spend time with him, holding him and singing to him. We could literally sit for hours doing just that, and he would be genuinely content; clapping his hands with a smile on his face. People always say that the eyes are a window to the soul...I see that in Lucas. It doesn't matter if he's healthy, happy, tired, sick, or hurting, I always see Jesus revealed in him." What a tribute to his life!*

This testimony is a powerful reminder to me of the irony that Lucas was not a punishment for poor choices, but a messenger of God's love. Although poor choices will almost certainly result in negative consequences, when we accept the gift of grace that Jesus offers us we are no longer condemned. The Old Testament law existed to reveal human weakness and to reveal the need for a Savior, but *there is now no condemnation for those who are in Christ Jesus* (Romans 8:1). The new life that Christ offers is not about keeping track of good deeds and bad deeds, hoping that the good stuff comes out ahead. It is about realizing our weaknesses, accepting His love and forgiveness, and working diligently to become more like Him.

As we have walked this journey with Lucas, I have often reflected on the life of Job. Job was a good man, *blameless and upright, a man who feared God and shunned evil* (Job1:8). His life was full of good deeds, right priorities, and great wealth, yet God allowed him to be tested through unthinkable loss. His material possessions were destroyed, all of his children and most of his servants were killed, and his body was inflicted with painful sores from the soles of his feet to the top of his head.

Sitting in a heap of ashes, the only "comfort" that he received from his wife was the recommendation that he give up his integrity, curse God, and die! Job had no one to blame and nothing to hope for. Just as I questioned myself and my integrity when Lucas was born, Job began asking God to show him what sin he had committed to deserve such incredible catastrophe. He asked God why he was ever born and why he should go on living.

God listened patiently as Job tried to make sense of his situation, and then God responded with a few questions of His own in chapters 38-40:

Who is this that darkens my counsel with words without knowledge? Where were you when I laid the earth's foundation? What is the way to the place where the lightening is dispersed? Can you bring forth the constellations in their seasons? Does the hawk take flight at your wisdom...or the eagle soar at your command and build his nest on high? Do you have an arm like God's and can your voice thunder like his? Then adorn yourself with glory and splendor, and clothe yourself in honor and majesty...then I myself will admit to you that your own right hand can save you.

This reproach brought Job to a position of utter humility, "Surely I spoke of things that I did not understand. My ears had heard of you but now my eyes have seen you" (Job 42:2-5).

Prior to Lucas, I too spoke of things that I did not understand. My life was about image...looking good and sounding good. I was raised in a Christian home, attended church twice every Sunday, lived in a Christian community, went to a Christian high school, and graduated from a Christian college. I knew scripture from memory and heard the stories of the Bible countless times.

My knowledge was abundant, but I lacked understanding. Lucas was a catalyst to my enlightenment. The helplessness that I experienced taught me to humble myself before God and man. Becoming aware of my sinfulness taught me that I would never be good enough to deserve God's love or bad enough to lose it.

My ears had heard of the Lord, but it was the gift of Lucas that opened my eyes to really see Him. It was the gift of Lucas that personalized God's sovereignty and grace, and it was the gift of Lucas that made me realize that basketball games are not what truly matter. At the end of the day, what truly matters is becoming more like Christ.

Seeing God at work through the life of Lucas has produced far more wisdom than years of *hearing*. He cannot recite scripture or inspire others with eloquent words, but his message has been loud and clear. His quiet lessons have caused the following poem to become very dear to me[9]:

> *I'd rather see a sermon than hear one any day;*
>
> *I'd rather one should walk with me than merely tell the way.*
>
> *The eye's a better pupil and more willing than the ear,*
>
> *Fine counsel is confusing, but example's always clear;*
>
> *And the best of all preachers are the men who live their creeds,*

*For to see good put in action is what
everybody needs.*

I soon can learn to do it if you'll let me see it done;

*I can watch your hands in action,
but your tongue too fast may run.*

*And the lecture you deliver may be very
wise and true,*

*But I'd rather get my lessons by observing
what you do;*

*For I might misunderstand you and the
high advice you give,*

*But there's no misunderstanding how you
act and how you live.*

The situations and events of our lives will shout to the deepest part of our souls louder than any speech or sermon. My mind had been filled with good and true information. God knew that a lecture on priorities or His grace and sovereignty would simply be filed in the archives of my mind, but He knew that Lucas would teach me things that would change the way I lived. I suppose that you could say that Lucas has been my sermon, and he has delivered it powerfully without ever saying a word.

Dear Lucas,

__T__he number "13" has become very special to me because it represents you. It's the day you were born—June 13.

Many people consider the number "13" to represent bad luck. Many builders of skyscrapers skip the number "13" when numbering their floors, believing too many guests would be uncomfortable staying or doing business on the 13th floor.

There was a time when I kind of bought into that logic. Not anymore! I view June 13 as a special day and, therefore, the number "13" has become a perfect reminder of the gift God gave us in you.

Most mornings I set my alarm clock for 6:13 a.m. The numbers "6-13" remind me to give my best for the day because I know that you have to give your best every day. Many times your brothers will yell out "6-13" when the numbers come on our television or on our car radio. They, too, give thanks for you. In fact, "6-13" is an active and constant reminder to our whole family to pray for you and to give God thanks for you.

I don't take little things like eating, reading, writing, running, talking and driving for granted. These are things that I get to do every day, and it is your life that encourages me to invest these abilities for maximum daily impact.

When I have to wake up earlier, I set the alarm in a sequence of numbers that add up to 13 or with the minutes that end in 13. For example, many times I will set the alarm for 5:26 a.m. because five plus two plus six equals thirteen. And, again, I think of you. Or, I'll set the alarm for 8:13 a.m. (I wish) because the number ends in 13, and again I think of you.

This ritual may seem silly to some, but it has become a significant part of my day, calling me to a higher standard each morning.

My day starts better when I think of you and puts things in right focus before my feet ever touch the floor. It is your life of perseverance, your competitive spirit, and your unconditional love that motivate me to strive for authenticity and to make a difference in the lives of others.

You inspire me, kid...and you do it without saying a word!

Trust in the Midst of the Storm

Reflections from a mother's heart
By: Darla Vander Plaats

Our morning was off to a routine start as Lucas and I drove the rural highways between our home and one of the many medical facilities that provided him care and therapy.

We were usually joined by three-year-old Josh, chattering the whole way, but today it was just Lucas and me. And I was soaking up the rare moments of silence in the van.

Lucas was still an infant and his car seat was positioned in its usual place, nestled between the two front seats on the floor. Although its placement didn't comply with safety standards, it was necessary for us. Lucas never went long without needing assistance and I had to be able to reach him easily and quickly.

For the moment, Lucas was asleep and in the quiet of my mind I began to ponder the strange and frightening turns my life had taken over the past several months. I began experiencing mental, emotional, and physical "turns" the moment Lucas was born and the stress of it was more than an occasional sensation or an overused cliché. For me, it had become a lifestyle.

There was emotional stress. I grieved for the child we had planned and hoped for, knowing that Lucas would never fit our original expectations. I never asked or planned for a child with so many problems and never envisioned the kind of lifestyle that Lucas brought with him. It wasn't long before I began viewing myself in a whole new way. I had become "the mother of a disabled child," as if it was the most defining thing about my entire life and, emotionally, that was difficult for me to accept.

With much grief came much guilt and the stress of it continued to build. Early on, Bob and I didn't realize that the feelings we fought were part of an acceptable and even necessary process. Instead, the guilt churned within us, suggesting that we didn't love the "imperfect" child we had been given. And it was something neither of us talked about.

There was mental stress. I had so much to learn in such a short time. Literally overnight, we were expected to know a flood of medical terms and procedures. We began working with a branch of the public school system that dealt with the special needs of children like Lucas, learning about Individual Education Plans, early interventions, and processes that I had never heard of before.

In addition to tracking the scheduling demands of in-home appointments, hospital and doctor visits, medication needs, and therapy routines throughout the day, I was determined to remain fully-attentive to the many joys and demands of our two healthy sons, who desperately needed me. My mind was in a constant spin cycle.

There was financial stress. The responsibility of handling the family budget wasn't a serious stress to me, being the accountant of the family, but our financial situation was similar to that of many young families. Bob was the primary bread winner, still getting established in his career and experiencing many moves and changes along the way. We had moved just months before Lucas was born and were still adjusting to a new set of financial circumstances.

Now, having a child with severe disabilities was a new financial stress for us to deal with: insurance deductibles and co-pays, increased travel for medical appointments, and hospitalizations which led to hotel and restaurant bills.

We encountered the need for nutritional supplements, which were not the least of our newfound expenses. The good news was that the added nutrients and calories helped Lucas maintain his weight and seemed to make him much more content. The bad news was that the stuff was expensive! Our insurance didn't cover nutritional supplements even if prescribed by a doctor, so our grocery budget took a hit.

There was physical stress. My days were consumed with maintaining the home, giving piano lessons, caring for Lucas and the rest of the family, and playing taxi driver. To be completely honest, it was often a strange sort of relief when Lucas was hospitalized because then I had the help of wonderful nurses and healthcare aides. They took care of Lucas while I was forced to let the rest of my duties go. I could just sit and cross-stitch, read, or sleep. They were rare moments of solitude, to say the least.

At home it was go, go, go all day long and the nights were rarely restful. Even when Lucas was feeling well, which wasn't often, he would wake up several times a night. When he was sick, I either bedded down in his room beside the crib or just held him in my arms while trying to catch a few moments of sleep in the recliner. All of this was exhausting enough, but what really sapped my energy was wondering if it would ever let -up. As I looked ahead to the coming days, weeks, months and years, I feared exhaustion to be a permanent condition.

The height of stress for me, I think, was in trying to act as though everything was fine. Maybe I wasn't covering nearly as well as I thought, but I felt pressured to wear a mask of composed competence. I tried to act as if nothing had really changed in my life; as if our family was no different than that of our friends or siblings. I had everything under control. But this confident facade was nothing more than a thin covering over the insecurity and anger that were looming just beneath the surface.

In that private place, driving the rolling highways, an emotional storm began to brew. Why *me*? Why *my* child? Why *my* family? What is going to happen? How am I going to keep doing this? On and on, the questions pounded and my feelings of grief, disappointment, helplessness, and fear were met with no immediate relief.

Most of the time, when such painful questions surfaced, I simply shoved them to the back of my mind until the chaos of life swept them away. But at that moment, when the only thing begging for attention was the very storm I was trying to avoid, it all washed over me and I was completely overwhelmed.

Romans 8:26 says, "We do not know what we ought to pray for, but the Spirit himself intercedes for us with groans that words cannot express."

If the truth of that verse ever applied to me, it was at that moment. In the midst of turmoil, God answered a prayer that I didn't even know how to pray by sending His Spirit to minister to mine in a powerful way. I had never experienced anything like it.

God began revealing precious and simple truths that brought healing to my wounded heart and peace to my tired mind. For the first time in months, I became aware of how much I had to be thankful for.

Even though our financial condition wasn't ideal, it was also not terrible and I began to realize how blessed we were to have good medical insurance which prevented us from accumulating the devastating medical debt that burdened other families in our situation. Feelings of frustration began turning to feelings of gratitude.

Once He had my attention, the Lord began showing me some things about my marriage. Bob was incredibly busy during those years, working hard to establish his career as a high school principal and I never questioned his commitment to either his career or his family. Sheldon High School, where he served, had some sort of activity scheduled nearly every night; from sporting events to music concerts, Bob was there for it all. He was absorbed in doing his job well and the students and teachers loved him.

I wanted him to succeed. I was proud of his accomplishments and I knew that he was having a positive effect on many lives. So why did it bother me? It bothered me because every time he headed out the door to an event, I was left home alone to care for our three little boys and to manage the details of our family. He loved me and was a loving father to the boys, but when the boys were young – before the basketball years – I longed for him to be a more hands-on father.

Part of me understood that it was the most efficient and effective arrangement – let him worry about his job and provide financial stability while I worry about the details of our home. It had worked well for us so far. In the meantime, I was starting to question whether it was really the best way, now that we had Lucas. Resentment grew as I witnessed Bob's good nights of sleep. He felt it was necessary in order to be effective at his job and I felt it was a built-in excuse to be removed from the reality of our situation.

Thankfully, in the quiet moments of revelation, God showed me a new picture of my husband. Bob had become my strong, dependable safety net. I was out there walking a tight rope, day by day, but I didn't have any real fear of falling because I knew without a doubt, that Bob would be there to catch me if things fell apart. He would be there to pick me up and put me back on my feet. I took a hard look at what life would be like without him as my supporter, helper, and friend. Again, I was moved to tears of gratitude.

Little did I know, as Lucas and I headed to the doctor that morning, that I was the one in need of healing. God shifted my focus in a significant way that day and for the first time in months I recognized what was *right* with my life rather than focusing on what was wrong. My circumstances had not changed during the fifty-minute drive, but my heart had come full circle, and my feelings of lack were replaced with an attitude of abundance.

Without a doubt, the healing touch of God was at work within me and if I had ever doubted His transforming power, I never would again. Praise God from whom all blessings flow!

Of course, God never stops working in our hearts and He still had work to do in mine. With newfound inner peace and stability, compassion began to flood my heart for those who were experiencing similar emotional bondage. Suddenly I was aware that Bob and I had a beautiful opportunity, if we were willing, to use our story to reach out to others.

In chapter fifty of Genesis, Joseph comes face-to-face with the brothers who beat him, stripped him of his clothes, and sold him into slavery. If anyone had the right to resent their life-circumstances, it was Joseph – and nobody would have blamed him for it. But Joseph looked into his brothers' eyes and said, "You intended to harm me, but God intended it for good to accomplish what is now being done, the saving of many lives" [Genesis 50:20]. Joseph chose to focus on the good instead of the bad, and because he did, God used him to touch the lives of many.

There is much debate in our society about babies like Lucas, whether their lives have value or not. The birth of Lucas caused me feelings of anger and disappointment and I found myself stuck in the stress of it for months, unwilling to see beyond my own discomfort. As difficult as it is to admit, there were times in those early months when I did question the life of Lucas. I loved him, but I wondered what purpose God could possibly have for him.

Thankfully, God began to reveal His purpose for Lucas over and over again. It became wonderfully clear that God was choosing to use our 'tragedy' for good, both in our lives and in the lives of others. But before God could make His purpose clear to me, I had to stop fighting my circumstances, stop trying to change them, and simply submit to His will. I had to trust that He knew best, that His plan was much better than mine could ever be. I had to put Lucas in His hands, and trust Him to use our family as He saw fit.

I imagine the storm raging inside me during the months following Lucas' birth was much like the storm that Jesus and His disciples encountered on the Sea of Galilee; waves crashing over the sides of the boat, lightening flashing, thunder booming, confusion and panic all around. But not Jesus. In the midst of chaos, Jesus simply rebuked the storm and the storm stopped. It was no more miraculous in the lives of the disciples thousands of years ago than it was when God calmed the storm in my heart, driving the highways of northwest Iowa.

I will always treasure the moments that Bob and I shared when Lucas and I returned home that evening. For the first time, we talked – really talked—about the presence of Lucas in our lives and we began to grasp the idea that God was going to turn something that seemed tragic into something more beautiful than either of us could have ever have imagined. We found our bearings. We found new purpose and new meaning. Most importantly, we began to trust.

Of course, there have been struggles since then. Lucas was not healed, life did not become easy. But the storm in my heart has not come back. Through medical emergencies, sleepless nights, disappointments and separations, the peace that passes all understanding prevails when I remember the day God calmed my storm.

Although the journey, so far, has been very different from what I imagined when I first learned we were expecting our third child, I know now that God's plan is perfect even when my circumstances aren't.

"For I know the plans I have for you," declares the Lord, "plans to prosper you and not to harm you, plans to give you hope and a future. Then you will call upon me and come and pray to me, and I will listen to you. You will seek me and find me when you seek me with all your heart" [Jeremiah 29:11-13].

God is waiting for us to cry out to Him in our pain and fear and frustration. He desperately wants us to seek Him in the midst of our storm so that He can prove Himself faithful. There is no judgment. There is no condemnation. There is no "are you kidding me!" There is simply grace and hope, and the wonderful knowledge that we can trust Him completely because He loves us perfectly.

My Little Lucilou,

I still call you that even though you are hardly little anymore. You've grown so much physically and yet remain so sweet and gentle, innocent and untouched by this world. How wonderful it would be if we could all be more like you.

You need so little to be content - a full tummy, dry clothes, a warm bed (but not too warm), music, and several catnaps a day. When these basic needs are met you are truly happy. Add in some individual attention from family members or Ruth, and your cup overflows!

Yes, maintaining your health is complicated, but your life is simple. Most of the things that seem so important to the rest of us, things that we chase after and fret about, mean nothing to you. You've got life whittled down to the basics: physical needs and positive, undemanding, uncomplicated relationships with people. The rest of it simply doesn't exist in your world.

All of that leads me to the most important thing I've learned from you the reality that I can trust God in this life while He prepares me for the next. You are a constant living reminder that this world is not where we belong, and you're a beautiful example of what it means to be in the world, but not of the world. I think we both know that we're not experiencing the kind of life that

God intended when He first created the earth. Sure, there is beauty and joy in this life, but there is also pain and sadness. It's all intertwined. Most every moment of joy is tinged with a measure of sadness and often times we find ourselves surprised by the presence of beauty in the midst of our saddest days.

We live in a fallen world, but we are blessed with glimpses of God's grace. Your life has provided many of those glimpses and has made me long for the day when we will experience our Father's best - together.

On that day, I believe I will become more like you than you will become like me. You will shed your physical limitations and live pain free. You will be able to communicate and express your every thought and idea. But I will also be transformed. I will shed the cares and concerns of this world and live as purely as you. I can't wait until I am given the ability to love people as sweetly as you do, experience joy as unhindered as you do, and trust as completely as you do.

Thank you for the wonderful gift you have given me, Lucas, a peek into eternity. I love you!

Mom

Unconditional Love

Every chapter and word of this book have sprung from my love for Lucas and a passion to assist him in fulfilling his life's purpose, motivating "normal" people to live extraordinary lives. I sincerely hope this "light from Lucas" will inspire and challenge you to live your one-and-only life to its fullest in red-hot pursuit of *your* purpose.

The ultimate conclusion of the light I have gleaned from Lucas is, and always has been, unconditional love. The mere existence of Lucas continually reveals the fundamental nature of love…love without condition.

I love Lucas and Lucas loves me. We love one another without strings and without expectations; just pure, untainted love between a son and his dad. It is said that love is the greatest gift. I believe that's true. The reason Lucas has been such a precious gift is because he has brought so much love to our lives.

Our world seems to be in a constant struggle to grasp the concept of "true love". We use the term so casually that it has nearly lost its significance. Although we easily express love and affection for our favorite sports teams, foods, articles of clothing, and vehicles, we find it difficult to express our love for one another.

There are many grown men and women who still long to hear the words "I love you" from their parents and, likewise, there are many moms and dads who long to hear these words from their children. How can such a simple task be so difficult? I believe it's difficult because it involves risk.

When crossing the "I love you" line, we enter uncharted territory and our minds begin playing games. "What happens if they don't say I love you back?" quizzes the doubter. "She already knows I love her, so why must I express it?" reminds the realist. So why *do* we need to express it? It is simple. We need to say "I love you" because the people in our lives need to know that they are loved.

More than 30,000 people commit suicide each year in the United States[10]. I believe this disheartening statistic exists because people have a love-void. Children are having children. Teens and adults alike are having random sex in search of love, only to find emptiness and disappointment.

Expressing genuine, appropriate love for one another is vital to growing healthy relationships. For many, expressing love is something foreign a job they simply don't know how to do. So let's explore the "duh-huh" of love expression.

The first and most straight forward option for communicating your love is to simply say it. "I love you." These three little words, when authentically uttered, break down walls, fill gaps, and provide the basis for healing and growth. Go ahead... you can do it! Say the words to your children, your mom and dad, your friends and relatives, and anyone else that needs to know you love them.

Once you have said it, write it. We all enjoy receiving written communication from someone special. Whether a handwritten note, an e-mail, text message, or a formal letter, the written word is incredibly meaningful and can be preserved for generations.

Anytime I receive a note of encouragement I file it in an "I'm okay" folder. Thus, when bad days come and people are unkind, I can open the file drawer, remove both notes☺, and read them as a reminder that someone loves me.

Say it. Write it. Now, say "I love you" with a touch. There are times when a pat on the back, an embrace, a gentle squeeze of the neck, or holding someone's hand communicates more effectively than words ever could. I have resorted to touch many times simply because I didn't know what to say. A timely touch can say, "I'm here and I care."

In John 13:1-5, Jesus says "I love you" by demonstrating humility:

> It was just before the Passover Feast. Jesus knew that the time had come for him to leave this world and go to the Father. Having loved His own who were in the world, he now showed them the full extent of His love. The evening meal was being served, and the devil had already prompted Judas Iscariot, son of Simon, to betray Jesus. Jesus knew that the Father had put all things under His power, and that He had come from God and was returning to God; so He got up from the meal, took off His outer clothing, and wrapped a towel around His waist. After that He poured water into a basin and began to wash His disciples' feet, drying them with the towel that was wrapped around Him.

Notice the words, "He now showed them the full extent of His love." Jesus taught many lessons, performed many miracles, and displayed many acts of kindness. Here, He humbled Himself to wash the feet of His disciples.

Communicating genuine love requires a certain amount of humility. This may be the reason our twenty-first century world has such difficulty expressing unconditional love. Humility is contrary to pop-culture. We have been taught to hold our heads high and to take pride in ourselves so that we will appear strong to others. Humility, on the other hand, may be thought of as weak.

Christ is all-powerful, able to wake the dead with a simple command, yet he took on the role of a servant in order to prove His love. Many of us need to humble ourselves and symbolically or physically wash the feet of the people we love. If Jesus could do it, though He was without fault, surely we can do it.

Our God-given emotions can also express love beautifully. Paul tells us in Romans 12:15, "Rejoice with those who rejoice; mourn with those who mourn." Great love is expressed when we sincerely celebrate the blessings of others or weep with those who are experiencing pain. Our culture, especially the world of politics, teaches us to cheer inside when others experience difficulty and to envy the blessings they receive, but scripture is clear that we are to truly desire the best for others. Our emotions are a powerful component of our internal love guage.

My final suggestion in this not-all-inclusive list of ways to show love is to forgive. Ephesians 4:32 says, "Be kind and compassionate to one another, forgiving each other, just as in Christ God forgave you." Many relational pains arise as a result of unforgiving, bitter hearts, but scripture reminds us that we are all in need of forgiveness. We must let go of injustice and move on.

When I was serving as a high school principal, two of my female students were involved in a nasty fight; punching, pulling, tearing, yelling, and crying. After some cool down time, I called them into my office in an attempt to discover the cause of such cruelty between *friends*. What I discovered is that the fight, and the emotion that fueled the punches, was due to a remark that had been made in the sixth grade! The remark, as I recall, was one girl telling the other that she looked bad in a bathing suit.

I sat there dumbfounded. Here were two high school juniors, fighting over a remark that was made some five years earlier. Now I was the one with the job of disciplining them for something that should have been resolved long ago. Give it up already!

If this were an isolated incident it may be a bit comical, but the sad commentary is that many adults are still suffering from comments or actions of long ago, simply because they are unwilling to humble themselves and offer or ask for forgiveness. Paul tells us to forgive each other as Christ forgave us. In other words, we don't deserve forgiveness, but Christ forgives us anyway.

Go ahead, forgive those who have hurt you and then write and tell me of your newfound freedom!

Whether you choose to express your love by saying it, writing it, touching it, serving it, rejoicing and weeping it, or by forgiving, just be sure to express it genuinely and without condition. For this is the true measure of love.

Lucas is limited in his ability to express love. He cannot write love notes or say the words "I love you" and he certainly cannot wash the feet of those he loves. Even so, he is quite capable of expressing emotion through the sounds he makes. I love his sounds. Through them, Lucas verbalizes happiness, anger, sadness, excitement...and even love. His sounds of "ooh" and "aah" may seem meaningless to others, but they are priceless to me. They are priceless because they are authentic. Every noise Lucas makes comes straight from his heart.

I have had the opportunity to hear many speakers and have given many speeches, but the best speeches, without question, are those that come from the heart. It is a great pleasure to hear someone who can move an audience from laughter, to tears, back to laughter, and then to reflection and action. It is a talent to be sure, but their speeches only have impact because they come from the heart.

Even though I love to sing, my family is quick to point out that I do not sing well. I fully realize that singing is not in my area of giftedness. However, my family will also point out that when I sing, I sing from the heart. It may not make me sound better, but it enhances their tolerance and makes people smile.

"Heart" inspires people. A vocalist may give a performance that is technically perfect, but if it lacks spirit, it is nothing more than notes on a page. Inspiration comes when a singer combines extraordinary talent with a heart of passion.

First Corinthians 13:1 says, "Though I speak with the tongues of men and of angels, but have not love, I have become sounding brass or a clanging symbol." In other words, talk is cheap. Words are just words unless they come from the heart.

Lucas is not articulate by the world's standards. But the messages of love he expresses through indistinct sounds is often more powerful than that of the best trained preacher using the most eloquent words.

Love and passion are the motivator and activator of the message!

Unfortunately, the world we live in has too many ways of defining love, most of which are grossly distorted and untrue. It is these misuses and exploitations of "love" that makes Lucas' authenticity so refreshing. There is not an inauthentic bone in his body. In fact, it would never occur to Lucas to use his affections to manipulate others or to be self-indulgent when it comes to love.

When I have the opportunity to address parents of teenagers, I remind them that boys will give "love" as a means to get sex, while girls will give sex as a means to get "love." The message is clear and simple. Parents of daughters, make certain that your little girl knows that you love her...authentically. Parents of boys, make sure that your son understands and respects the true meaning and source of love.

This age-old battle between the worldly exploitation of love and love's divine intention is quite possibly the "tipping point" between a purposeful life and a life of wasted potential.

It boils down to a matter of focus. Each of us has the choice to focus our talents and gifts on personal satisfaction or on benefiting others and the decisions we make about how to use our abilities stems directly from a focus of the heart.

The focus of God's heart is perfectly clear, "For God so loved the world that He gave His one and only Son that whoever believes in Him shall not perish but have eternal life" [John 3:16]. God has one son...Jesus. He chose Jesus, who is without sin, to bear the sins of the world so that you and I could have eternal life in Heaven. God's heart is focused on us...the prize of His creation.

God has one Son. I have four. I believe that I have a heart for others, yet I cannot begin to think about sending one of my sons to their death for the faults of others.

Whether I can comprehend it or not, Christ says that this is how we are to love. Before He departed this earth He said, "A new command I give you that you should love one another as I have loved you. This way the whole world will know that you are my disciples" [John 13:34-35]. Christ was ridiculed, beaten, and put to death for us. Can God be serious?

Yes, God is serious.

He wants us to die to ourselves and to live for Him. If that means ridicule, beatings, disabilities or even death, so be it. Life on earth is temporary. Life with Christ is eternal. It's a matter of *heart*!

Love's true meaning provides me much comfort regarding the life and purpose of Lucas.

Lucas is patient...through needles, surgeries, seizures,

the awkward stares of strangers, and constant poking and prodding that is so often necessary for his care.

Lucas is kind...readily giving second chances and smiling in spite of the sometimes inadequate efforts of those he depends upon.

Lucas does not envy or boast, and he is not proud. Lucas is Lucas. His humble life encapsulates love, because the purpose of his life is for the benefit of others, not himself.

Lucas is not easily angered and he keeps no record of wrongs. Lucas has every right, according to the world's standards, to be angry, to have pity parties and to hold people's actions against them. Instead, he claps his chest and screams through a tracheotomy that he loves life and those around him. When I observe Lucas' resilient behavior, I have to ask, "What's my problem?"

Lucas does not delight in evil but rejoices with the truth...bringing out the best in people: doctors, caregivers, brothers, casual bystanders, and his mom and dad.

Lucas always protects...displaying his love and joy for family, special friends, and those responsible for his care. His facial expressions and physical behavior never depict a boy who has been cheated by life. Instead, his face says, "Thanks for loving me."

Lucas always trusts. Wow, does he ever! He has to trust. He is fully dependent for nourishment, personal care, and his overall well-being. His life has been built on trust. Because of the special love Christ showed to those with special needs while He was on earth, I believe that Lucas knows, and trusts, his Risen Savior and Sovereign God in a very personal way.

Lucas always hopes...to walk, run, and talk. I am confident that his hopes will be realized when he meets Jesus face to face. In Heaven, every one of Lucas' tears will be wiped away and every disability restored. Darla and I long to see him in Heaven...what a day that will be!

Lucas always perseveres...Many doctors have given us reasons for Lucas to give up on life, but Lucas has continually shown an incredible will to live. He has always persevered through seizures, through needles, through conspicuous stares, and through his daily, routine obstacles. His perseverance motivates me to keep striving!

1 Corinthians 13:10 says, "But when perfection comes, the imperfection disappears." Jesus Christ is perfect. This world is imperfect; you, me, a multitude of sin, and even the pain of Lucas' disabilities. God sent his perfect Son to save a world burdened with defects.

When I picture Christ on the cross, with His arms outstretched, I see the heart of our Father God saying, "I love you this much." When I stop to consider the powerful impact Lucas has had on my life, I can hear God saying, "I love you this much."

I believe Lucas was created to reveal God's love and glory, and I praise God for giving Darla, our boys, and me the gift of Lucas. We love him and he loves us...unconditionally.

The greatest expression of love is accepting Jesus Christ as our personal Lord and Savior. By accepting this great gift, we experience the absolute love of our Creator. Our response to the Father's love should be a life committed to Him, to His

Will, and to the advancement of His Kingdom. And the most excellent way to show our love for the Father is to love those He has put into our lives.

Lucas has helped me to understand unconditional love, and for this I am eternally grateful. Through many years, and many tears, I have loved Lucas just as he is. I don't know what tomorrow will bring, but I have faith and hope in our Lord to carry our family through. And I have a precious and powerful love for Lucas that can never be taken away.

Now these remain: Faith, Hope, and Love. And the greatest of these is LOVE!

LIGHT FROM *lucas*

His Light
SHINES ON

We'll be with you soon...

If Darla and I could have foreseen our journey with Lucas on the day of our marriage in 1983, I believe we both would have run. We wouldn't have seen the blessing, only the pain. We wouldn't have embraced a divine plan, instead we would've only seen disruption to our preferred journey. There's no way we would have stayed. I'm positive we would have not simply walked the other way, but we would have sprinted in the other direction. Lucas didn't fit our vision of the desired future.

The vows for better or for worse, have real meaning and much practical application. As Darla said in the promotional video for *Light from Lucas*, "Everybody has something. And if you haven't had something—a struggle or a challenge—you will."

Pretty uplifting vision for marriage and life, wouldn't you say?

But it's true. And don't just take it from Darla, but take it from Jesus when He assured us in John 16:33, "In this world you will have trouble."

I emphasize this every time I'm given opportunity to present on the *Light from Lucas.* Everyone has a story. Why? Because we weren't designed for this side of eternity. Therefore, you and I and Darla and Lucas are going to have trouble. I get the opportunity to share Lucas' story, our story, in speeches and in this book; but that said, I am fully aware everyone has a story.

When I shared the original *Light from Lucas* manuscript to potential endorsers and to others who would offer constructive critique, I was stunned when a successful person, who hails from a wealthy family, commented that Lucas' story was his story. He went on to say that he doesn't really know nor is close to anyone with disabilities. But Lucas' story is definitely his story. Wow.

Just as Darla remarked, everybody has something. It doesn't matter what the bank balance reads or what the title is, everybody has a story.

As you will undoubtedly see in the following pages, Lucas' story speaks to and impacts so many. Yes, it speaks to parents and to families who are gifted with a special-needs life. But as Lucas' story peels back the masks of pretention, it will speak to many. And if you'll permit, it may even speak to you.

This is my hope and prayer as I, with the help of Lucas' family, write *Light from Lucas...His Light Shines On!*

The original *Light from Lucas* was published in 2007 when Lucas was 13. At that time, our home was in Sioux City, Iowa. Hans was in his first year of college; Josh was a sophomore in high school; Lucas was being served in Sioux Falls, South Dakota (about 70 miles from Sioux City), at Children's Care Hospital and School (CCHS); and Logan was a fourth grader.

The 15 years since *Light from Lucas* was first published may not be that long, but there were many transitions in our family in that time.

Fast forward to November 2021. Darla and I now live in a suburb of Des Moines, Iowa, and we are grandparents. Hans and his wife, Courtney, have been married for two and a half years. They are parents to a daughter, Caroline, and are pregnant with their second child. They, too, live in the Des Moines area. Josh graduated from college and graduate school, earning a Master of Business Administration, and resides in Columbus, Ohio. Logan, too, has recently graduated from college and is living in downtown Des Moines. A lot has happened in each of our lives during these 15 years, but this is Lucas' story.

So let's talk about Lucas...

In spring 2012, Darla and I decided to move from Sioux City, Iowa, as I was leading the ministry, *The FAMiLY Leader,* in the Des Moines metro, and the three-hour (one way) weekly commute from Sioux City to Des Moines and back was taking a heavy toll.

Before making the actual move, however, we needed to ensure that Lucas' exceptional needs would be met in an exceptional manner.

Hoping to find a new home for Lucas, I called the president and CEO of *ChildServe.* Years before, while serving as president and CEO of Opportunities Unlimited, I served on statewide and national committees with the leaders of *ChildServe,* which has an impeccable reputation of serving special needs children and their families with unparalleled excellence. If we were to move to Central Iowa, we wanted *ChildServe* to serve as Lucas' home.

Our request was made, on behalf of Lucas, and we were quickly informed that *ChildServe* had one opening remaining in the northern Des Moines suburb of Johnston, and they were reserving it with Lucas' name. Wow. God's timing and provision were obvious. After 12-plus years of driving the 70-mile journey from our home in Sioux City to Lucas' residence in Sioux Falls, we were now going to be separated by a mere ten minutes.

Lucas received excellent care via the *ChildServe* team and medical community. His only emergency came in the Summer of 2014. It was in the early morning of *The FAMiLY Leader's* annual Leadership Summit, where we had several headliner speakers for the day keynoted by none other than New York businessman Donald Trump.

That morning, Lucas pulled out the tracheal tube that greatly assisted his breathing via his tracheotomy. Once the Respiratory Team was notified of Lucas' decision to dislodge this seven-year mechanical intervention, they went to great lengths to reinsert without success. Thus, they immediately ordered an ambulance to rush Lucas to the Emergency Room so the tube could be surgically reinserted.

Upon observation, the doctor noticed that despite the tube's absence, Lucas was not incurring any respiratory distress. Therefore, he decided Lucas may know what he's doing and ordered him hospitalized for a couple of nights to ensure he wasn't in need of this tracheal tube. Much to everyone's surprise, Lucas never again utilized a mechanical tracheal tube.

After a long history of constant medical emergencies and hospitalizations, this would be Lucas' last until...his last. And this emergency was on Lucas' terms. He was done with something he no longer needed nor desired. As a result, his physical appearance was more natural, while site infections subsided and breathing treatments reduced. It was a win/

win on every level – so much so, the respiratory therapy team began wondering how many more kids could do well without these foreign devices in their airways.

Darla passionately continued her advocacy and knowledgeable involvement in Lucas' care. I credit Darla and the *ChildServe* team as the primary reason for Lucas' prolonged life (remember, this little guy wasn't supposed to live for two days, then not two weeks nor two years – he was now 28 years old).

Darla's relationship with the lead nurse, in fact, prompted the nurse to contact Darla for consultation in mid-November 2021, regarding recent observations of Lucas. No one could pinpoint the cause, but Lucas wasn't himself. While his vitals were in the acceptable ranges, he appeared out of sorts and lethargic.

We didn't know it yet, but Lucas' life on this Earth was coming to a close.

As we reflect on this time and look at the pictures of our visits over the tough COVID years leading up to 2021, we see something now that we didn't allow ourselves to see at the time. For months, Lucas just wasn't responding to us the way he had when he was younger. The smiles were few and farther between, and when we did get one, it was just a quick flicker, a shadow of the way he had smiled before. Most of the time we got no reaction to our arrival or anything we did while we were there. We chose to believe that it was his medication, or that he wasn't feeling great, or it was...honestly, it was easier not to think about it.

ChildServe, to their credit, had been trying to prepare us. Prior to COVID, we met with a kind doctor. He explained to us that Lucas had been having seizures his entire life. Each seizure had an effect, and the cumulative impact of those seizures was both devastating and lasting.

Lucas' neurologist, in response to Darla's repeated requests for better medications, ordered a video EEG done on him. This took place in October of 2019. When he looked at the results later in Darla's presence, he pointed out that Lucas was seizing almost constantly, even when there was no outward sign of it. Unfortunately, he said, there was no medication that would make a difference for Lucas' situation.

ChildServe kept prodding us to sit down and think through our desire for level of medical intervention in the case of an emergency. We humored them and had the discussions and got an order in place. All of this probably should have given us some idea that others were seeing something happening – but it really didn't. Lucas had beaten the odds so many times, he had been brought so low and then had come roaring back so often, that we just couldn't imagine another outcome.

There was a process going on for years, but particularly in 2019, 2020, and 2021. The words came recently as Darla and I were talking in retrospect – "a slow fade." That realization brought sadness, but there was also a gift of grace that became beautiful and fitting. And it happened simultaneously on several levels.

Lucas never did say a word, but when he was young he had a lot of personality. His smile lit up a room. The twinkle in his eye was irresistible. His giggle drew smiles every time. There were many things he couldn't do and many things that meant nothing to him. But there were a few things that gave him great joy – car rides, loud music, his radio toy, Krispy Kreme donuts, Starbucks strawberry Frappuccinos, ice cream, his brothers jumping over him, sneezes, and the "I Love Lucas" song. Those things would always get a great reaction from him – smiles, laughs, and his signature clapping his chest. These were simple things, and it gave us great joy to provide them for him. We probably sang that simple "I Love Lucas" chorus to him tens of thousands of times.

Over the years, however, most of those things diminished. When he got his tracheostomy, it cancelled out the giggle. Over time, his swallow mechanism deteriorated, and we had to stop giving him solids and then liquids until he was solely tube-fed. COVID took away the possibility of car rides. Little by little the joys of life were removed, and even those that remained failed to get the same reaction. The Lucas we knew was fading away.

This next part has caused me – and probably even more Darla – a certain amount of guilt. It was just recently that we were able to see it in a different light – as a gift of grace. The natural progression, the gradual lessening of parenting responsibilities that happens with "normal" children, didn't happen with Lucas. Typically, a growing child gradually increases in competence and ability and gradually takes on more and more responsibility for him or herself. You never stop being a parent or caring deeply for that child, but eventually your responsibility for him or her ends.

With Lucas, the increase in competence never happened, and the need never lessened. In fact, it was magnified many times over a typical child. We had to find a balance over the years, giving up some of the responsibility to CCHS and *ChildServe*, but never being free of that connection, that bond, never wanting to be free of it or to let go of the responsibility that was rightfully ours.

When Lucas moved into a nursing home in 2016, the need stepped up dramatically, and for those two and a half years, even though our baby, Logan, was now out of the house and we were technically empty nesters, we were very much involved parents to Lucas. We spent countless hours with him during that time. When Lucas was later moved back to *Child-Serve*, there was a sense of relief and release of that heavy responsibility, and we were ready for it. We were ready to have a more normal level of responsibility for our age and the ages of our kids. When COVID forced the changes to our visits and schedules, it was probably inevitable that there was a further letting go – a fading of the connection and pull that we always felt toward Lucas. We recognized it, and frankly felt a mixture of relief, and guilt for feeling relief.

Now we realize that there was a providential measure of grace in the slow fade. It would have been so much harder at earlier times in his life to say goodbye. The slow fade, however, gave us the grace to start letting go.

By November 2021, though Darla and I were still slow to see it, the slow fade was reaching its end. Lucas' lethargy was worrisome, and after listening to the lead nurse, Darla suggested we try restoring many of the familiar activities that had been limited during the COVID restrictions. Immediately, *ChildServe* agreed to Darla's recommendation (this, in part, is what makes them good – they listen).

The very next night, Darla and I picked up Lucas for a Friday night van cruise around Des Moines. I lifted Lucas into the copilot seat, started up the van, and then turned up the music...really loud. Immediately, Lucas arched his back and shaped his mouth as to commence singing. This would be his last song.

As much as Darla and I tried to sing, to turn up the volume of the radio, to drive in sport car fashion...Lucas couldn't reciprocate any further. All of his songs had been sung.

Two days later, Darla and I were again given permission to take Lucas home after church. We thought for sure being at home, Lucas would bounce back to a normal equilibrium. Nope. Again, Lucas remained rather emotionless only to play his music occasionally. The good news is Lucas' brothers, Logan and Hans, along with Hans' wife, Courtney, and daughter, Caroline, were able to join us for Lucas' final Sunday home. And I was able to take one, final nap alongside Lucas in our Murphy room.

Things continued to remain stagnant and in decline throughout the week without any obvious reason as to the cause. While Darla and I were scheduled to be at a co-ministry fundraiser that Friday evening, Darla decided not to go and instead to be with Lucas. I stopped by Lucas' residence briefly to see Lucas and to chat with Darla before proceeding to the fundraiser. Throughout the evening, I had an uneasy feeling regarding Lucas' state.

All in all, Lucas had a decent night, as his mom slept next to his bedside in the room's recliner. Darla returned home at approximately 6:30 a.m. so she could get some extended sleep, while I took my Saturday morning shift to be with Lucas. Lucas appeared to be resting peacefully, assisted by oxygen, and not in any immediate danger. We watched the beginning of the Illinois at Iowa Hawkeye football game in his room.

All appeared to be well. The Hawkeyes were scoring, and Lucas was resting quietly. He was stable enough that I decided to enjoy a bike ride on an unusually beautiful fall day, while Darla returned to *ChildServe* to be with Lucas. Not only did I enjoy a 33-mile bike ride, but Darla also returned home to spend the night at home to get some needed sleep.

When Darla adjourned to take a bath before going to bed, however, she let me know that she was in a funk. Something wasn't right.

While Darla and I both went to sleep in our home, we were awakened at 2:30 in the morning by the lead nurse in charge of the overnight shift. We both noticed the anxiousness in her voice. Lucas was still comfortable, but something was wrong. Immediately, we got in our vehicles to be by Lucas' side. After being briefed on Lucas' vitals and status, Darla made the decision to stay, while I returned home around 4:00 a.m.

At 4:42 a.m. Darla texted me that Lucas had a seizure and that she would be staying with him.

At 7:21 a.m. I texted Darla for update. She replied immediately that Lucas' doctor was en route to see him. Wanting me to be there with her to discuss Lucas' condition with his doctor, I rushed out of the home to head back to Lucas' residence.

Lucas' doctor was straightforward. Lucas had pneumonia, and if we chose to keep him at the *ChildServe* facility, we would be making the decision of "comfort care." In her opinion, their current oxygen and antibiotic treatment would no longer suffice. For Lucas to have a chance, he needed intravenous antibiotics and fluids that could only be administered via hospitalization.

A few months earlier, Darla and I visited with this same doctor regarding life-saving interventions for Lucas in case he encountered a life-threatening event. We were briefed in detail on all the options. This discussion prepared us for what we were now facing. While Darla and I wanted to do what we could to preserve Lucas' life, we did not want heroic measures and mechanical interventions. This little boy has been through enough and, frankly, the potential return benefit on these "all in" measures was minimal, if any at all.

Upon consultation with Lucas' doctor, Darla and I gave the green light for an ambulance to be summoned to take Lucas to the emergency room for assessment then for hospital admission. As we awaited the arrival of the ambulance, I told Lucas that I wanted him to fight, but it was also ok to let go and to go home with Jesus. Darla and I then prayed over him and asked God for His will to be accomplished.

When Darla and I were allowed back in the emergency room, the ER doctor charged with his care provided a frank diagnosis. Lucas had pneumonia in both lungs with fluid buildup outside of the lungs creating additional pressure. His high heart rate and rhythmic breathing indicated that he was not responding well to the current antibiotic and oxygen regimen. With a more aggressive antibiotic treatment, we would know within 24 hours if he was responding and turning the corner or...the doctor finished with his opinion that it didn't look good.

After the doctor left us, Darla quickly remarked, "He doesn't know Lucas."

Darla's assessment was based on experience. Lucas beats the odds. He always had, which naturally led us to believe he would again.

After a dinner from Panera Bread in Lucas' hospital room, I gave him one more kiss on his forehead, told him and Darla goodbye, and headed for home to tend to our seven-year-old puppy, Chelsea. Even as I returned home that Sunday evening, my gut instinct believed that Lucas would turn the corner. This instinct allowed my thoughts to go forward to the week ahead and all that needed to be accomplished in our short Thanksgiving week at *The FAMiLY Leader*.

After a few phone calls regarding the upcoming week and Lucas' updates, I adjourned to bed with my cell phone ringer set to on. As I went to bed, I considered the doctor's words regarding the 24-hour timeframe to assess Lucas' response. I determined that if Lucas wasn't responding, I'd recommend we bring him home with us for his transition to Heaven.

At 4:27 a.m. the next morning, my phone rang. I sprang out of bed, my head racing with two quick thoughts...Lucas is in trouble or Darla needs me to relieve her so she can get some sleep.

Darla's words were brief, "I think you better get down here."

I immediately got dressed and rushed to my truck, making my way to Lucas' hospital in downtown Des Moines.

It turns out Darla had fallen asleep in Lucas' room only

to be awakened by several medical professionals rushing into Lucas' room. His vitals were crashing. His heart was slowing. His oxygen saturation was plummeting. And just as the lead doctor began barking orders, Darla interrupted them to ask how they were going to intervene. At that time, a nurse reminded everyone that Lucas had a DNR (do not resuscitate) order.

Darla's only request was that they keep Lucas alive until I arrived to say goodbye. The doctor responded that he believed Lucas was making the decision for everyone.

Darla picked up her Bible and began reading Psalm 23 over Lucas. As she read scripture, she comforted Lucas and assured him, "We'll be with you soon."

I rushed safely from our home in Grimes towards the hospital in downtown Des Moines, hoping and praying that I would arrive to say one last goodbye. As I approached the 73rd street exit on Interstate 235, approximately ten minutes from the hospital, Darla called again. Lucas had passed.

While I instantly grieved Lucas' passing, I was also provided an immediate peace. There was no audible voice from God. Instead, my spirit was immediately comforted with an impression of the reality that I wasn't needed for Lucas' transition to Heaven. My job and Darla's job, as parents, were finished. Lucas needed only Jesus. No one else and nothing else, not even parents would do. Only Jesus.

On November 22, 2021, at 4:40 a.m. Lucas went home... with Jesus.

Best Friends

You'll remember Ruth in the "There Are Angels Among Us" chapter. Ruth and Lucas had an inseparable bond. Ruth proved to be invaluable to Darla and me and all four of our boys, especially Lucas. Ruth spent much time with Lucas at our home, at Lucas' home, and most importantly, in her heart. Lucas' life had a deep impact on Ruth's life. And, yes, Ruth's life had deep impact on Lucas' life. They were in every possible way best friends!

The following is Ruth's final tribute to Lucas, followed by a letter to Lucas:

I first met Lucas when he was around five weeks old. Darla came to the Sheldon High School office to talk to Bob and set Lucas in his car seat on the counter. I went over to keep an eye on him, and he turned his head and gave me a big smile. Ever since then he has had my heart.

Shortly after, Bob and Darla asked me to watch the boys when they were invited for a night out. I was taught how to give breathing treatments, meds, and how to provide any other needs Lucas had, and he was so patient with me. Always a smile, always acceptance, always grace.

We spent so much time together over the years just hanging out and enjoying each other's company. When he was younger and I could hold him in my arms, he would often utter a deep sigh. We were content just being together. I would often talk to him about how one day he would walk, run, and talk, and we would share many stories about his life. He would sometimes giggle at this, and I firmly believe he understood exactly what I was saying.

The pandemic put a hold on our visits, and I wasn't able to see Lucas for over 18 months. He was on my mind daily, and I missed being able to spend time with him. Just three weeks prior to Lucas' passing we were finally able to see each other, and it was such a blessing to hear him belly laugh not just once, but three times. I am so grateful to God for that memory and cherished gift.

I have learned more from Lucas in the last 28 years than from anyone else, although he never uttered a word. The verse from Philippians 4 that states in part, "For I have learned, in whatsoever state I am, therein to be content," exemplifies Lucas's attitude in life.

He lived unconditionally. Unconditional love. Unconditional acceptance. Unconditional joy. I remember Darla saying at one time that when we go to Heaven, we will become more like Lucas than he like us.

Thank you, Lucas, from the bottom of my heart. I will be forever grateful for the gifts you have given, forever blessed by your presence in my life, and forever thankful to God for you.

Dear Lucas,

And we know that in all things God works for the good of those who love him, who have been called according to his purpose (Romans 8:28).

You are precisely who God intended, Lucas... I love you.

I am privileged to write you, Lucas. From the moment God placed you on this earth, you have captured my heart. Although you have no words, you have impacted my life in a heroic way that is nearly indescribable. I anticipate our future in Heaven someday, when you will share your thoughts with me. I want to hear them all!

We have made many memories over the years that I will forever treasure. The depth of your eyes tell me so much; they show your soul.

You find joy in the small things, like just being present. There is nothing that is insignificant to you, Lucas. I am forever astonished by the thrill you find in simple pleasure. You are swift to offer a heart-warming smile and have the ability to fill my heart by just relishing the moments when we are together.

You've spent hours upon hours on my lap laughing, singing, and being together. Some of our favorite songs are "Row-Row-Row Your Boat" and "I Love Lucas." One day you will sing in God's palace, Lucas. I can't wait to hear your voice!

I'll never forget our long walks in the park in Sioux Falls, being filled with wonder by watching the birds and also the leaves blowing in the wind. Whenever I am with you, I feel near to God; this a true testament of your character.

The countless life lessons you have taught will never be forgotten. You have shown me unwavering perseverance and how to accept each and every situation. You have made known the importance of loving unconditionally. It is no secret that your true joy comes from within, by fully living the life God created.

You motivate me, Lucas. You inspire me to fulfill God's will in my life. You grant me vision and encourage me to honor God and serve those around me. I am so proud of you.

Thank you, Lucas, from the bottom of my heart. I will be forever grateful for the gifts you have given, forever blessed by your presence in my life, and forever thankful to God for you.

I love you, Lucas!

Boys to Men

Darla and I are so proud of our boys and their response to Lucas. God provided Lucas with older and younger brothers, hemming him in front, alongside, and behind by his brothers. These brothers truly loved their brother Lucas, and Lucas truly loved his brothers.

The following are the eulogies shared by each of Lucas' brothers at Lucas' memorial and celebration-of-life service. Our second son, Josh, provided a powerful kickoff to Lucas' eulogies, while our youngest son, Logan, provided a touching tribute to Christian community. Our oldest son, Hans, summed up the brothers' tributes by stating, "Being Lucas' brothers was the greatest honor of our lives."

Darla and I choked up with emotion and with much pride as we witnessed these boys, one by one, give powerful testimony to Lucas' life. Grab a Kleenex and take it in.

Josh

Lucas was a constant in our lives for 28 years. Logan and I do not remember life without Lucas. Hans might remember Luke's grand entrance. The helicopter rides. The frequent hospital visits. We as Lucas' brothers have now entered a new chapter of life: Life without Lucas.

Some of my first memories of Lucas were on our living room floor. Lucas was fragile. That was obvious. Nevertheless, we are brothers. Even though typical roughhousing was off-limits, we had to get as close as we could. Often, while Mom was preparing dinner or we were watching TV as a family, Lucas would lay on the floor, on his favorite blanket. We would take turns running and jumping over Lucas. The ground would shake, and Lucas would erupt with laughter. After each jump, Lucas would laugh so hard that we would have to wait for him to catch his breath for the next jump. It was a silly game. But Lucas loved it. So we loved it.

Another childhood memory included Sunday mornings at Sunnybrook Church. Lucas was an astute critic of Sunday morning church services. If Lucas enjoyed the music or the sermon, he would sing along, clap his chest, and offer his form of encouragement. If Lucas was not satisfied with the offering, he would make it known. We were always watching. Waiting. If Lucas wasn't enjoying the service, one of us brothers would be ready to take him out of the sanctuary and into the halls of the church. I would often find my way to the gym to shoot some baskets, careful not to let the ball hit the ground. I did not want to be caught out of church playing basketball. We were always excited when it was our turn to take Lucas on a walk.

When I was in third grade, Lucas moved to Children's Care Hospital and School (CCHS). I remember being very confused when Lucas moved away. Mom and Dad explained it to us. But we were just kids. We didn't understand why our brother

BOYS TO MEN

could not be at home with the family. Sundays at Sunnybrook turned into Sunday afternoons in Sioux Falls. After church, we would load into the family Suburban and drive 90 miles north to Sioux Falls to see Lucas. Once there, we would take a cruise with the family that would include Cinnabon, Krispy Kreme, Dairy Queen Blizzards, or a Starbucks Frappuccino. Being his father's son, I don't think Lucas had a choice, but he loved ice cream.

One of the things I'll miss most is Sunday afternoon after church. Lucas would go to church with Mom and Dad and then spend the rest of the day at their home. Lucas would nap with Mom, play with his Playskool Rockin' Radio, and watch football with the family.

These are just a few of the many memories that we shared with Lucas. This book is full of lessons learned from Lucas. I want to share some of the lessons that Lucas taught his brothers. We didn't always realize it, but Lucas shaped us. We learned so much from Lucas, but I'll keep it to a top three:

1. Life is fragile: One look at Lucas and you knew he was fragile. Everyone that met Lucas could see that he was fragile.

2. Try your best: Lucas couldn't do some of the most basic things. From walking and talking to going to school and playing sports, Lucas showed us that every single thing we can do is a gift. Tomorrow isn't promised. Don't waste the time you are given. Give maximum effort.

Don't just go through the motions.

3. Majors are major, minors are minor: Lucas had a way of helping you realize what is important. If we were/ are ever stressed about school/sports/job/girls, Lucas served as a reminder of what's really important. Our dad put it well: Lucas had a way of centering you.

We will not stop thinking of Lucas. And I think he will continue to center us. We will continue to learn and grow because of the lessons Lucas taught us. We didn't really talk about it, but we knew that there was a good chance that one day, we would have to eulogize our brother. It doesn't make it easier to say goodbye. Parents are not supposed to bury children.

The week after Lucas' death and the preparation for his funeral left a lasting impression on me. We are so lucky to have the parents that we have. Lucas was so lucky to have the mom and dad that he had. Their faith is inspiring. I imagine having a kid like Lucas provides many "make or break" moments for your faith. It is clear that the experiences provided by Lucas strengthened their faith. That faith is the reason that we are still celebrating Lucas.

We believe that Lucas is now home. In a new body. No more tears. No more disabilities. We are so proud of Lucas. My mom said before that in Heaven she thinks that we will be more like Lucas than he will be like us. I think she is right.

Logan

It was a privilege to grow up with Lucas. I don't fully understand how he was able to do it all these years, but I am forever grateful. Grateful to God for the gift of Lucas, grateful to my family for showing what it takes to love and care for someone like Lucas, and grateful to Lucas for being an incredible brother and friend. He laughed in the face of adversity, he showed so much strength, even in times when he had so little, and he never lost his joy in the little things. Whether it was having him punch me for giggles, our family car rides, or just lying with him watching TV; the problems in life seemed so small in his presence. He was a great role model and I hope to cherish these lessons throughout my life.

The week of the funeral, Hans, Josh, and I found it important to acknowledge and thank a few of the people that made this journey possible. Lucas had an incredible support system that not only was there to care for him, but also was there to support the rest of the family in whatever ways they could. Between grandparents, family members, and friends, it always felt like we had people to turn to in times of hardship. One friend turned out to be more of an angel for this family:

Ruth Klein. Ruth was always there in a moment's notice to do whatever was asked. Ruth never asked questions and never hesitated. Her steadfast dedication not only allowed for the best care for Lucas and us, but also gave Ruth and Lucas the opportunity to grow a loving, deep relationship that was a joy to watch.

And of course we want to acknowledge our parents. God gave Lucas parents that showed him endless love and fought for him every step of the way. Their love and strength for Lucas has always been inspiring. They've faced the toughest decisions imaginable and endured the scariest situations a parent can face. Yet they've never lost faith or sight of where our hope lies. Mom and Dad instilled a faith in Lucas, and in us, that makes his life a celebration and his death a bit less painful. We know where Lucas is; we know he is rid of all earthly chains. I can't wait to see Lucas again and hear of his many adventures in his new body.

Hans

Lucas was, in a way, the most grateful person I've known, in the sense that being grateful is appreciating things, not taking them for granted.

Given Lucas's disabilities, he wasn't able to do many of the things that make up a "normal" life. But where he could take part, Lucas enjoyed things in a way the rest of us can barely imagine.

He loved music. All kinds. Country, Christian, older stuff. He loved it when you turned the music up loud. Loved being in a place like this, listening to people sing. Even, somehow, loved listening to our dad sing. His favorite toy, by a mile, is that rock and roll radio. Went through countless numbers of them. It was music that he could control. And he did. If he wanted to listen to just one particular song, he'd hit that toy mercilessly to get through the lineup and back to the song he wanted to hear.

He also loved car rides. Cruising. To most of us, driving is something mundane, something to get through. To Lucas, it was a thrill. He could be on the move. A favorite memory for all of us was getting Lucas positioned in the car, everyone ready, and then turning the ignition. Lucas would hear that engine and jolt up, huge smiles and laughs, a roar of his own, get so excited, and almost out of breath before we'd even started.

He loved his family, his friends, the many people who cared for him. He had his ways of showing that. The excitement at the sound of a voice he knew.

He loved just being around people – especially around people that seemed to be in the moment, playing some game or whatever it was. Which is why I think he especially liked being around little kids. Loved to be around them as they played. He'd laugh when they laughed. He'd even laugh when they cried. Just loved being around them.

He loved life, he certainly fought for it. Doctors said he wasn't likely to live for two weeks...two months...two years.

Lucas showed them. But it wasn't easy. The seizures, the close calls, the difficult medical treatments, they took their toll, but Lucas kept fighting his way back. It wasn't his time.

But it's OK that this time it was. It's sad, but it's also such a fun thing to think about him now. We'll likely all enjoy Heaven plenty, but maybe not quite like Lucas. No more disabilities, no more suffering. The things he's probably trying right now, for the first time, with that new body of his!

It's such an honor to be Lucas's brothers, and among the greatest gifts of our lives. Being around Lucas, you couldn't help but want to be better. To be more like him. More genuine. More enjoyment of the simple things. More grateful. He was a wonderful person who blessed so many during his life. So let's celebrate him.

A Mother's Love

I remember asking Darla the Tuesday before Lucas' Friday memorial service if she wanted to say a few words. She replied that there was no way she would be able to get through any remarks. Thursday morning, the day before Lucas' service, she told me that she believed that God laid on her heart to honor Lucas with a eulogy.

Expressing gratitude for a son's 28-year life is hard. Darla requested prayer for God's sustaining grace as she expressed her love for her son and thankfulness to her God. God answered her/ our prayer as she delivered a most poised and touching tribute.

When she finished, there wasn't a dry eye in the sanctuary. As you read her tribute below, you'll quickly grasp why.

Those of you who know me know that I am not a public speaker. My inclination, in this time, was to do lots of things behind the scenes, but to leave this part to the rest of the family who are good at it. But yesterday I woke up with the thought that I can do better. Not for me. Not for anything or anyone else. But for Lucas – I can do better. I need to do better. And there was a message that I had running through my mind and my being. That message is gratitude.

I'll be honest, I had had this feeling that I would never truly be able to celebrate Thanksgiving again. These memories – Lucas' passing and preparing for his memorial service – would be too painful, too hard. But as I have reflected, going through pictures and the memories that they triggered, I have been gaining perspective. The truth about this journey with Lucas is that most of the time you don't really reflect, you keep moving – you do the next thing that has to be done. But now we have to stop, take a step back and look at the bigger picture and hopefully gain a new perspective.

As I have been doing that, it struck me that so many of the big events of Lucas' life, which were almost always medical crises, happened at just the right time. In his first two years, he had five helicopter rides, three of the times were because he had simply stopped breathing. Each time I was not alone with Lucas, but Bob was right there with me to help, both practically and emotionally, to get us through it. I could give many more examples.

And then this – Lucas's transition. If I really think about it, it happened at just the right time. Three years ago, legislation was enacted, largely because of Lucas' situation, that radically changed the way medically fragile young adults get served. Lucas lived long enough to see that law changed, and he lived long enough to enjoy the benefits for almost three years. And there are many more young people who are enjoying the benefits now and into the future. That's a great legacy. Then there is the fact that Bob and I have been, just in the last ten weeks or so, in Alaska, Colorado, Florida, Minnesota, Washington, D.C., and Texas, and I can't help but think – what if we get that call when we're hours away and struggling to get back here. Now we were both home, able to be close and responsive when it really mattered. And we got to spend extra time with Lucas in his last ten days. It hit me that the timing, over Thanksgiving week, was actually perfect. In fact, I am pretty sure that going forward, Thanksgiving is going to be my favorite, the time when I can remember Lucas' legacy with a joy and with a depth of meaning that, I hope, won't fade as the years go by.

You see, there is so much gratitude that is threaded through Lucas' journey. The other day Pastor Eric was at our home, and something he said or asked made me think about this. For years, Lucas was in Sioux Falls, at Children's Care, and we were in Sioux City. We visited pretty much every Sunday and lots of times in between Sundays. In my memory, the great majority of those visits went this way: Lucas greeted us with joy. Each time he lit up when he saw and heard us, he expressed his gratitude for our visit in his own unique way. He enjoyed the hours that we spent together. Our goal was always to kind of wear him out – that when we had to leave, we would settle him into his bed and watch him roll over and close his eyes for a nap, so that it didn't feel as bad to walk out and leave him... again. But whether he fell asleep or he didn't, he never did anything, in all of those years, that put extra guilt on us. There was some guilt that we put on ourselves, but he never added to that in any way. He showered us with gratitude at the beginning of the visit and never retracted a bit of it at the end. Lucas was very good at gratitude.

Another aspect of gratitude in Lucas' life was the gratitude we felt, and still feel, for the many, literally hundreds of wonderful people who in different ways served him and his diverse needs. Of course, there is Ruth, who became, just because of her huge heart and her enduring bond with Lucas, such a big part of his life. It was such a comfort to Bob and me to know, for many years, that almost every Saturday morning Lucas was going to get a visit from Ruth, and we knew that he was so blessed by the time that they spent together. But there were also so many teachers, nurses, aides, doctors, social workers, etc. who served Lucas so very well through the years. I especially want to single out the *ChildServe* community that served Lucas from 2012 through 2016 and then welcomed him back and served him for the last almost three years. What an incredible group of people. We really can't say enough about the care and, yes, love that he received on a daily, even hourly basis from folks that did their very best to bless him and make sure that he was as comfortable and cared for as he could possibly be.

There is gratitude for the family that God gave us to walk this journey with us. As you have seen, God gave Lucas some very special brothers, and Bob and I some very special sons, and we are so grateful for the part they have played in his life and ours. God gave Lucas a one-of-a-kind dad, and me a one-of-a-kind partner for the journey. I can't imagine better. And our extended family, our TFL (The FAMiLY Leader) family, and our church family all have helped us immeasurably through the years. We are grateful beyond words.

There is gratitude to God. Again, sometimes we need to take a step back to gain perspective. I didn't always feel grateful. In fact, I often had big questions and not many answers. But the perspective God has given me today is that, as they say, we were never alone in this. He has walked with us through every step. He has given us what we needed when we needed it. It has been a long, difficult journey. There has been pain and suffering. There has been confusion and heartache. But at the end of it, I can honestly say that I am grateful that God chose us to walk the journey with this very, very special young man named Lucas. And I can tell you that there were blessings all along the way, even if it has taken years in some cases to really see them.

Finally, and most importantly, there is gratitude for the hope that we have in Jesus. This week we have all been clinging to and trying to focus on the picture of Lucas enjoying his new home. Imagining him without that chair, walking, running, talking, singing, and eating. As good as your Thanksgiving feast was yesterday, Lucas' was better, and today's is just as amazing and tomorrow's and the next day's. We have that hope. I was able to tell Lucas just before he passed, "We'll see you really soon." Because Jesus defeated death, we have the assurance that Lucas is not gone. He is not gone, and we have not lost him. We know where he is, and he is better than he has ever been.

We are grateful to each of you for being here today and for your own part in Lucas' journey. We hope and pray that you will be able to see and celebrate the blessings that God has given you through Lucas.

A Father's Love

Over the years, I have given several eulogies, but none tougher than delivering a eulogy for Lucas. Darla and I were well aware that most likely this day would come, but you're never really ready. Lucas is our son, and we love him dearly.

Many commented that it's extra tough when death is out of order. Parents aren't supposed to bury children children are to bury their parents. That said, Darla and I reminded all that this is the right order. While Lucas has great brothers, we are his parents, and he would always be in need of us. As painful as saying goodbye to Lucas is, we didn't want him to be without us.

Below is my eulogy.

When Lucas was a newborn, Darla and I lived in Marcus, Iowa. Early in Lucas' life, one of Hans' four-year-old friends was over at our home. Hans was excited to introduce his new baby brother, Lucas, to his friend. After looking at Lucas, who was sporting a larger than normal head, a frail body, and a skinny neck, along with a red oximeter light on his index finger, Hans' friend quipped, "Your brother looks like E.T."

While the comment may have stung, it was an accurate depiction.

"E.T." inspired the song "Turn On Your Heartlight," sung by Neil Diamond. It is a song we associate with Lucas to this day, because in very tangible and intangible ways, Lucas is responsible for turning on our, and many other, heartlights.

Today, as we celebrate Lucas' life, I believe in the spirit of Lucas, it's only fair to be authentic and transparent. From the time of Lucas' birth to the time of Lucas' death, there have been many questions...but, one timeless question...the question is, "Why?"

Why the seizures? Why the life flights? Why the many near-death experiences? Why the disabilities? Why the blood draws, why the IVs, why the alarms, why the rescue breathing, why the ambulance rides, why the tracheotomy, why the feeding tube, why the full spinal fusion surgery, why can't he talk, why can't he hug, why can't he live at home, and the list goes on and on.

And, if we're totally, gut-wrenching honest, the biggest why question of all is, "Why us?"

These questions of why have flooded our time with Lucas. Yes, we have faith. This is why we are here today. And, yes, we have hope and assurance because of our faith, but seriously, why? Why Lucas? Why us? Our question is, "Why?"

Not why, but "Who?" was the question the disciples asked of Jesus. They inquired of Jesus, "Who sinned?" when they came upon the blind man. In their cause-and-effect understanding, the obvious disability had to be a result of sin. And yet, Jesus said, "No one sinned." This statement rocks our world. But then it begs the question, "Why?"

And, being Jesus, He gives the answer. In John 9, He states that this is so God's mighty works might be displayed.

Are you kidding me? Lucas' disabilities and this guy's blindness display God's mighty works?

I don't believe for a second that God's mighty works are displayed in Lucas' disabilities. However, I do believe God's mighty works have been revealed in you, in all those who have responded with love, care, and generosity to Lucas. Yes, we've seen God's mighty works being displayed in our collective response to Lucas' disabilities.

I've seen God's mighty works displayed through Lucas' mom. I recently told Darla that observing her being a mom and a grandma is like watching a masterpiece. Her tireless devotion for her boys and now her grandchildren from a servant's heart, I believe, showcases God's heart for mothers and their offspring. Regardless of society's influence, being a mom is the highest call for mothers.

Darla is exceptionally bright, an avid reader, and a very quick learner. This is what propelled her to be summa cum laude, to graduate with honors, and to pass her CPA exam on her initial try. She's smart and accomplished. Yet, she traded it all in to be a mom.

Her aptitude was needed for Lucas. And she gave it. She studied and learned all she could about Lucas' diagnosis and about prescribed medications and treatments. She questioned doctors and medical professionals. Her questions, her intellectual insight, and her mother's instinct were needed for Lucas to maximize his potential and his purpose.

Not only is Darla smart, she's also a fighter. Darla grew up on an Iowa farm. She nursed calves, caught fish, broke her arm in the hayloft, and played with her brothers and her boy cousins. While some watch *Yellowstone*, Darla lived *Yellow-*

stone. Simply put, she's tough.

Darla put this fierce combination of intellect and toughness to use as she advocated and fought for and fought alongside Lucas. God's mighty works were displayed through Lucas' mom, Darla.

I've seen His mighty works displayed through Lucas' brothers. You've already read the tributes of Lucas' brothers. Wow, need I say more? These three young men and their faith, their strive to give their best, and their kindness and charity towards others have been forged by life with Lucas. It is through these boys where Lucas' light will shine on...from generation to generation.

I've seen His mighty works displayed through Ruth. As Logan mentioned in his eulogy, I'm not sure how we make it through the trials of Lucas' life without Ruth. Ruth's biggest gift was she was present. She was present with Darla. She was present with me. She was present with each of our boys. She was present with Lucas.

Ruth's heart was motivated out of love for Lucas and for our family. And through that love, she sat with us, she rode with us, she stayed with us, she changed careers, and she moved to be with us. Ruth was the exemplar of Christian community. She didn't take a class or read a book on how to demonstrate Christian love. She just saw a need and responded with her heart.

God's mighty works were displayed through Ruth.

I've seen His mighty works displayed through Lucas' caregivers. These trusted heroes stepped in the gap and embraced Lucas as one of their own. They laughed with Lucas.

They cried with Lucas. They were with us through the good times, the bad times, and the uncertain times.

It is their love, their devotion, and their dedication which leads us to honor them, all of them, as Lucas' pallbearers.

God's mighty works were displayed through Lucas' caregivers.

And we've seen God's mighty works displayed through a very generous country that values the dignity and purpose for all life. Lucas' life was given added days and much value do to a most generous country. Even, as Darla pointed out, when we encountered obstacles, our leaders responded with a collective heart that values life...all life.

This is why so many say Lucas' life impacted so many. It wasn't Lucas' disabilities, it was God working through you and so many others who responded to Lucas' special needs that vibrantly displayed God's mighty works.

This is why Darla and I can say we give thanks and lift up praise for the gift of Lucas. When you think about this... Wow. Just flat-out WOW!

As I mentioned this past week to The FAMiLY Leader's Pastor to the Board, Monte Knudsen, "Isn't it ironic that life's most powerful sermons aren't spoken...they're tangible, they're depicted by love in action?"

It gives credence to that famous poem, "I'd rather see a sermon than hear a sermon any day."

Lucas' life and all those who responded to it in agape love, the highest level of love, delivered a most powerful sermon that will have Kingdom impact for generations to come. To this I say, and I believe God will say, "Well done!"

On Lucas' last Sunday, Darla and I were in Lucas' room when the decision to call the ambulance was made. While waiting for the ambulance, I took the opportunity to talk to Lucas. I told him I wanted him to fight, but it was also OK to break the chains of this life and to go home to be with Jesus.

The next morning in the hospital Darla awoke to Lucas' last emergency. Medical teams rushed in as Lucas' vitals were crashing. Darla's only request of the medical team was to keep Lucas alive until I arrived from home. As I rushed from our home down the interstate towards the hospital, Darla called me to let me know that Lucas was gone.

After we shared a 28-year cry on the phone, Darla shared with me that she read Psalm 23 over him as he was taking his last breaths. As Darla read, I believe Lucas heard, "The Lord is your shepherd, Lucas. It's ok. Run to Him. You're going home. Jesus has prepared a place for you."

As you heard, Darla assured Lucas, "It's ok. It won't be long. We'll be with you really soon!"

And just like Jesus healed the blind man, Jesus healed Lucas...at 4:40 a.m. while I was passing the 73rd street exit. Please hear my heart in this: As much as I wanted to be there for Lucas' final breath and to say, "Goodbye," I was not needed. Jesus was all Lucas needed. And Jesus is all you need and all I need. No one or nothing else will do. At 4:40 a.m. on Nov. 22, God revealed the mightiest of works when He healed Lucas with a new eternal body through the gift of His son, Jesus.

Darla and I frequently discussed what going to Heaven

would be like for Lucas. We can only imagine Lucas grabbing on to Jesus' hand and Jesus saying to Lucas, "Well done, Lucas! Your time on earth is done. Let's run! Let's jump! Let's dance! No more tears, no more disabilities, no more wheelchairs, no more feeding tube. The table is prepared. Go eat! After you're finished eating, go ahead, take a ride across the moon!"

Wouldn't you just love to see him now? If God opened the heavens for us to get just a glimpse of Lucas now, we'd have to shield our face and turn away, because Lucas now reflects the glory of God. And, if we could see him, we'd quickly realize we're the ones still in chains while Lucas is free. And the only way for us to break through is, just like Lucas, we need to run to Jesus.

This is why we give thanks. This is why we give praise. This is why our grieving is temporary, but our joy is eternal.

So, our prayer today is that we'd – you and me – choose to turn on our heartlight, be inspired afresh by the light from Lucas, and then pop the clutch by embracing Matthew 5:16 and letting our light shine so our Father in heaven is glorified and many come to the saving grace of Jesus.

I love Lucas, yes, I do. Yes, I do. Yes, I do. He's my buddy, buddy...buddy, buddy, buddy. I love you. I love you! I love you, Lucas. (Singing)

One More Lesson

As you probably can assess by the tributes of Ruth, Lucas' brothers, and Darla, Lucas' memorial service honored God, honored Lucas, and pointed all to Jesus. Our goal with Lucas' service was to give praise for and to celebrate the gift of Lucas. The service delivered...

Recently a friend called to inform me that he was returning from a funeral of a business associate. He said the service was long and pointless. This celebration of life merely retold stories, some funny and some more business natured, of one man's life. He then went on to say that Lucas' funeral has become the benchmark for him regarding all funerals. It was powerful. It was meaningful. It showcased God's mighty works through a life too many find useless and meaningless. In short, Lucas' celebration-of-life service had impact.

Ten days prior to Lucas' passing, Darla and I had dinner with some dear friends. These friends had been on a journey to Israel spearheaded by The FAMiLY Leader and orchestrated by Darla. If you've ever been on a "come and see" missionary journey to Israel, you know that your fellow journeymen become like family. These friends are that kind of friends.

Our dinner was intentional. We desired to celebrate a relationship that appeared to be coming to an earthly end. Our friend was diagnosed with cancer shortly after our 2017 journey to Israel, and the battle to fight this disease was coming to an end. Although placed in hospice, she still could get out for brief stints with the assistance of her husband.

The dinner was blessed. Words of appreciation and feelings of love were shared. So were stories that brought needed laughter and cleansing tears. Saying goodbye to someone you love is tough. It is only through our faith that we find joy. Seeing Jesus face-to-face with every tear and cancer cell being wiped away, with the promise of reuniting with those who go before us, provides us the hope and the courage to move forward.

As we transparently discussed this four-year journey with this life-altering and likely life-ending cancer, our friend expressed to us that she and her husband had resolved early on to "walk well." Their desire was to point people to life, an abundant and an eternal life, in this earthly circumstance that was robbing life and ushering in death.

While Darla and I organized this dinner to be a blessing to friends amid a tough time, we were the ones leaving blessed. The testimony of choosing to "walk well" was inspiring and proved to have major significance to what Darla and I were about to face.

One week after this dinner, Darla and I were coming face to face with the reality of Lucas' pneumonia, hospitalization, and pending death. Immediately, Darla recalled our friends' words, that we're going "to choose to walk well." Doctors, nurses, emergency personnel, sons, family, friends, and several extended and attached communities would be watching. This is where the rubber meets the road as it relates to our faith. We desired Lucas' life and death to be a testimony.

I believe it was these words and this focus that allowed

the days encompassing Lucas' illness, death, and funeral to be such a blessing. I've been part of deaths and funerals that tear families apart, where the words and actions are far less than "walking well." This was not the case for Lucas' transition. His death didn't separate, it brought us together.

Lucas was good at bringing our family together. Whether it was car rides or garage visits or hospital stays, Lucas had a knack for bringing our family together. The Thanksgiving week of Lucas' passing, our family was going to be separated. Hans and Courtney and Caroline would be staying in Central Iowa due to the lateness of Courtney's pregnancy. Logan was going to travel to Northwest Iowa to be with extended family. Darla and I had plans to be in Columbus, Ohio, to celebrate with Josh and his girlfriend, Daniela. All that changed when God brought Lucas home on the Monday of Thanksgiving week. Suddenly, we were all together for Thanksgiving and for the whole week. Lucas brought us together one more time.

While grieving his passing, we sincerely celebrated his life and joyfully praised God for his new life with Jesus in his new body. Walking well isn't always easy, but it is a choice and a focus that greatly blessed us during the toughest of times. And this choice was inspired by a friend whose funeral we'd attend only days after Lucas'.

Hans mentioned in his tribute to Lucas that the reason saying goodbye to Lucas hurts so much is because we loved him so much. His life impacted ours greatly, and in many ways, was a magnet for our family. The void we feel and will feel is real. While our faith and our joy are real, our hurt and our pain are real as well. This is love.

Darla and I wanted Lucas' service to be authentic with praise and worship to God while honoring Lucas and pointing all who attended or who would watch to Jesus. Thus, we planned it with these goals in mind.

Lucas' casket was ushered to the front by a team of pall-bearers representing *ChildServe* and Lucas' friends and house-mates. Our immediate family followed as the congregation joined in singing "10,000 Reasons." Specifically, we wanted to praise God with the lyrics:

> *Bless the Lord O my soul*
> *O my soul*
> *Worship His Holy name*
> *Sing like never before*
> *O my soul*
> *I'll worship Your Holy name*

And we wanted to affirm our faith with the song's lyrics:

> *And on that day*
> *When my strength is failing*
> *The end draws near*
> *And my time has come*
> *Still my soul will*
> *Sing Your praise unending*
> *Ten thousand years*
> *And then forevermore*

This song is one our favorite worship songs, as it communicates our enduring faith on this side of eternity and in eternity: 10,000 years and forevermore.

The welcome and the official commencement of the service were given by good friend and pastor, Erick Voelker. Erick concluded his welcome with the official reading of Lucas' obituary:

Lucas Harlan Vander Plaats met his Lord and Savior, Jesus Christ, cheek to cheek and face to face, where every tear and disability were wiped away on November 22, 2021, in Des Moines, Iowa. He passed peacefully while his mother, Darla, read Psalm 23 to him. He was 28 years old.

Lucas was born to his parents, Bob and Darla Vander Plaats, on June 13, 1993. Lucas was born with a very rare brain disorder, Partial Pachygyria Lissencephaly, resulting in life-long physical and mental disabilities requiring 24-hour care. While severely limited in "normal" activities, Lucas loved car rides, loud music, the Iowa Hawkeyes, his roommates, hanging with his special friend, Ruth, and all who served in his care.

Lucas' life displayed the glory and mighty works of God, clearly seen in the love, nurture, and support of many. In addition to his family and Ruth, Lucas was blessed by the ministries of Children's Care Hospital and School in Sioux Falls, South Dakota, and ChildServe in Johnston, Iowa.

Many blessed and impacted Lucas' life, and, in return, Lucas blessed and impacted many, many lives. Ruth Klein, who met Lucas when he was an infant, modeled this through a special friendship. Ruth's love for Lucas and her heart to serve forged an enduring bond, revealed through timeless smiles. Ruth's friendship to Lucas is a tangible testimony of how God uses the weak to teach the strong, while displaying Jesus' heart for those with special needs.

Welcoming Lucas into Heaven's gates are grandparents,Esther Granstra and John and Kathryn Vander Plaats; along with uncles, Harlan and Bradley Vander Plaats, and Aunt Barbie Vander Plaats. Continuing to live out the lessons learned from Lucas are his parents, Bob and Darla Vander Plaats of Grimes, Iowa; his siblings Hans and Courtney (Brandt) Vander Plaats of Des Moines, Iowa, Joshua Vander Plaats of Columbus, Ohio, Logan Vander Plaats of Des Moines, Iowa; his niece Caroline Vander Plaats; and his special friend, Ruth Klein of Sioux City, Iowa. Lucas' light on earth is also reflected in grandparents Dixon and Char Granstra of Rock Valley, Iowa, along with his uncles, aunts, cousins, friends, and caregivers.

We praise God for the gift of Lucas' life and the gift of eternal life. We are picturing him running, jumping, talking, singing, and maybe even dunking as he enters into his Savior's courts with praise!

After the welcome and the reading of the obituary, the congregation joined in the singing of "The Goodness of God." It was important for Darla and me to praise God as a reminder to ourselves, our family, and our friends of God's goodness through the life and trial of Lucas. Take these lyrics in...

I love You, Lord
For Your mercy never fails me
All my days, I've been held in Your hands
From the moment that I wake up
Until I lay my head
Oh, I will sing of the goodness of God

And all my life You have been faithful
And all my life You have been so, so good
With every breath that I am able
Oh, I will sing of the goodness of God

I love Your voice
You have led me through the fire
In the darkest night
You are close like no other
I've known You as a Father
I've known You as a Friend
And I have lived in the goodness of God

And all my life You have been faithful
And all my life You have been so, so good

With every breath that I am able
Oh, I will sing of the goodness of God

The brothers followed with their tributes, as you read in an earlier chapter. Darla and I were greatly blessed by their tributes – specifically, Joshua stating, "I want that faith", Logan highlighting Christian community by Ruth and how she blessed Lucas and our family with her tireless love and servant's heart, and Hans commenting on how Lucas made you want to be better and that being his brothers was one of the greatest honors of their lives.

Following the brothers' tribute, we planned the song "Blessed Be Your Name" by the Newsboys. The following lyrics were our point of emphasis:

Blessed be Your name
On the road marked with suffering
Though there's pain in the offering
Blessed be Your name

Every blessing you pour out
I'll turn back to praise
When the darkness closes in Lord
Still I will say

Blessed be the name of the Lord
Blessed be Your name
Blessed be the name of the Lord
Blessed be Your glorious name

You give and take away
You give and take away
My heart will choose to say
Lord blessed be Your name

Following this reassuring song was my and Darla's parental tribute to Lucas. As mentioned earlier, Darla is not a fan of being in front of an audience. But God prompted her to give a message on gratitude, and from now on Thanksgiving would be a special holiday for us. My focus was to emphasize the mighty purpose of Lucas' life. It was arguably the toughest public message either of us ever gave, but we are so glad we did. We wanted to honor God by recognizing the gift of Lucas.

The song Darla and I chose after our tribute was none other than "I Can Only Imagine." Darla and I can only imagine Lucas in the presence of his Savior. No more disabilities. No more pain. No more seizures. Able to run, to walk, to dance, to talk. We can only imagine!

After Pastor Erick's message of Lucas' life forging the faith and impacting the lives of Lucas' family, friends, and care-givers, the congregation concluded in praise with "Amazing Grace" and "I Raise a Hallelujah."

The service concluded with the congregation singing, "I love Lucas, I love Lucas, yes I do, yes I do. He's my buddy, buddy. Buddy, buddy, buddy. I love you. I love you."

I don't believe there was a dry eye in the sanctuary as Neil Diamond's "Turn On Your Heartlight" played over the sanctuary's speakers. As family and friends exited, they were given a Krispy Kreme glazed doughnut and a balloon. Once outside, the couple hundred in attendance gathered in a circle, sang one more time "I Love Lucas," and then let the balloons go, signifying Lucas' eternal freedom.

As I replay in my head and write out the details of Lucas' service, I get overwhelmed with joy. It was such a powerful service – so powerful that so many have requested a link to take in the service either again or for the first time.

Three cameras were rolling to livestream and record Lucas' service in one of the most high-tech churches in the Des Moines metro. An error was made, however, in pushing one button. This powerful service would be reserved for only those in attendance.

While disappointed, Darla and I believe this unintentional error highlights one more lesson from Lucas. For Lucas to impact one's life and for one's life to impact Lucas' life, you had to be there. There was no phoning it in or zooming it in for Lucas. To know him, you had to spend time with him.

In our high tech and high rush world, we get accustomed to quick hits and drive-by relationships. This didn't suffice for Lucas. He couldn't text nor talk on the phone. The only way to experience Lucas and for Lucas to experience you was to be there.

One of my best friends from college called me a couple of days after Lucas' service. He commented to me that after attending the service he wished he would have known Lucas more. I quickly assured him Lucas was a tough kid to get to know. It took time. Lots of time. This deep impact from Lucas' life was reserved to Darla and me, his brothers, Ruth, and his caregivers and housemates.

Joey was one of Lucas' housemates who was always there. Living one room down from Lucas and sharing a bathroom between the rooms, Joey and Lucas became close. While severely limited physically, Joey is a bright young man who can verbalize his thoughts, and his smile is infectious. Joey took on the responsibility of keeping an eye on Lucas.

A couple of nights after Lucas' funeral, Darla and I journeyed one last time to Lucas' room to pack up his belongings. While there, we asked one of the team members how Joey was doing. She informed us that he was taking Lucas' death pretty hard, making sure everyone who came into the house knew he lost his friend, Lucas.

Before Darla and I left, this team member informed us that Joey would like to see us. We went into Joey's room and began talking to him. Joey was sad, making us sad, so I thought I'd lighten the mood by asking Joey if he remembered the song we sang to Lucas.

He immediately said, "I Love Lucas!"

I commenced singing with Joey joining in, and at times, being ahead of me with the words.

Joey knew Lucas' song because he was there with him and for him. I believe this is what Jesus had in mind when He commanded us to love our neighbor as ourselves. I think Jesus wants us to know our neighbor's song, to keep an eye on them, and to be there for them. All of this takes time. We have to be there.

The Mighty Works of God

The clue phone was ringing, and no one was picking it up. It was 1999, Lucas was five years old, and I was presenting to a joint appropriations committee lead by Republican and Democrat legislators in the state of Iowa. My presentation was on behalf of the Governor's Council I chaired. The entire focus of the diligently prepared proposal was to revamp Iowa's delivery system for people with special needs based on two fundamental tenants: 1) Philosophically right and 2) Economically smart.

Our ultimate goals were to maximize an individual's independence and potential with avenues for safe, healthy, dignified, and purposeful living. Not only did we believe this represented Iowans' value for being philosophically right, but we also believed this model to be economically smart. Keeping people in their most natural and independent environment would be a cost savings. While some individuals need 24-hour institutional care, many do not. And 24-hour institutional care is expensive.

The other prevalent issue we wanted to address was the age restriction on receiving most appropriate care. To control costs and to heighten predictability, the arbitrary age of 21 became the standard for access to the full complement of services. If you lived past 21 or if your disability occurred after age 21, in Iowa at the time, your options ranged from bad to none. The needs didn't go away only the eligibility for service.

We aimed to change this continuum of care based on predictable system thinking to an array of options based on individual need. Highlighted in our presentation were facts, based on current data, that individuals and families would be given better service and maximum independence resulting in best outcomes at a better value to Iowa's taxpayers. It represented the proverbial win/win.

While delivering this PowerPoint presentation with stories and data, I simultaneously looked around the room assessing leadership acumen, specifically the "bias for action" meter. As my eyes intentionally went from legislator to legislator and bureaucrat to bureaucrat, I determined the clue phone was ringing with the information we presented, but it was way outside their innovative grasp to pick it up.

After the presentation and the subsequent question and answer period, I left the heavily adorned State Capitol room to the marble hallway. Immediately to my surprise, the chairman of the committee came rushing up to me, stating that was the best prepared and well laid out presentation ever given to the committee. I could tell in his eyes he was enthusiastic about what he just heard, but I could also sense in his tone that his hope for advance was dim.

This is when I went to my truck, picked up my flip cell phone, and pulled out its antenna to call Darla. After explaining to her that the presentation went well but the outlook for action wasn't bright, she asked me what I was going to do next.

This is when I flippantly told her, "I'm going to run for governor."

She responded with three words, and they weren't, "I love you." They were, "Are you nuts?"

Systems are purposed for control and for predictability. Systems control the universe eligible for costs, thus giving bureaucracies predictability. While systems are good for uniform delivery and cost control, they suck at meeting individual needs and being philosophically right.

And while I didn't become Iowa's governor, Darla and my advocacy for people with special needs never ceased. That said, we never dreamt that in 2015, nearly 20 years after my advocacy for this system change, our voice would still be needed. And now our voice would be needed for Lucas. His situation was in the proverbial crosshairs.

Ironically, many of the same players that occupied the seats of power were still in charge. The appropriations chair, the one who applauded my presentation years earlier, was still the appropriations chair. Iowa Gov. Terry Branstad made a comeback to win election, again, and was in his second term in his second stint as governor. Due to his comeback, he brought back the same director of Human Services. The good news was I knew the players. They knew me. And they knew Lucas.

Immediately Gov. Branstad acknowledged the lack of progress and granted Lucas an emergency one year of additional eligibility to be served with excellence via *ChildServe*. This one year would buy us time to engage the legislative and bureaucratic process for needed system change.

These processes are complicated involving many moving parts. This recommended change to the system required a willing governor, an agile Department of Human Services, a supportive legislature, and a highly regarded service provider. *ChildServe* readily agreed to be the service provider, and Gov. Branstad put his full weight behind achieving this change. Governments don't move fast, however, and Lucas' one-year emergency provision was coming to an end.

Darla and the *ChildServe* professionals began searching for best placement for Lucas. To say quality options were slim would be a vast understatement. There were no good options close to the Des Moines metro and only substandard options hours away from our home. We – Darla in particular – were feeling the pressure.

Another Des Moines Metro couple was facing the same dilemma for their son, Aaron. Out of options, Aaron's mom took to the press to tell their story. *The Des Moines Register* ran a frontpage story entitled, "No one will take my child." In this published story, Aaron's mother, Carol, passionately laid out the very dilemma we were facing with Lucas. It was the cry for help so many parents and families face when their child runs out of options.

Lucas and Aaron were running out of time, and us parents were running out of options. The reality was setting in. Lucas and Aaron were going to have to leave *ChildServe* as soon as another willing provider was secured.

Finally, a nursing home in the Des Moines metro agreed to accept Lucas. The tour was disheartening. Although the staff and residents were friendly and the facility was clean, this placement was a far cry from our goal of philosophically right. Frankly, it was the exact opposite. It was philosophically wrong. Placing a 22-year old male in a geriatric setting where *Jeopardy* and *Wheel of Fortune* were the highlight was inappropriate.

It was also medically dangerous. While the staff of this nursing home desired to serve Lucas well, his needs and his demands were way beyond their preparation and professional scope. One prolonged and unmonitored seizure would be the unfortunate end. Not only would Lucas be dead, but the state of Iowa and this specific nursing home would be liable. Part of my ongoing argument with elected officials and bureaucrats was why allow a devastating circumstance and an expensive payout be the spark for change? If we know better, we should do better, before something bad happens.

All this said, our options, along with Darla and I, were exhausted. Lucas aged out of a system designed to meet his needs. Now he transitioned from a place he called home, where his needs were met with excellence, to an unfamiliar setting not designed for his needs or his age. It was an emotionally devastating time for Darla and me.

Our anxious assumptions were quickly realized. The staffing levels weren't even close to adequate for Lucas' needs. Lucas had a tracheotomy, a feeding tube, and a major seizure disorder. He required breathing treatments, time sensitive seizure meds, repositioning, and transferring from wheelchair to bed to chair and vice versa. This was just to keep him safe and to meet his baseline healthcare needs.

Due to this inadequate placement, Darla spent many of

her days in Lucas' room monitoring his needs and many nights sleeping in the recliner next to Lucas' bed. The situation was physically and emotionally draining.

Our goal was to get his basic healthcare and safety needs met first before addressing the recreation of going outside, engaging in activities for enjoyment and stimulation, listening to his music, and watching his tv/movie/sports selections.

Through no fault of their own, the staffing level wasn't adequate. The staffing wasn't consistent. The training and expertise Lucas required was simply non-existent at the nursing home. All in all, this was a bad placement. And way too many families like ours and young adults like Lucas were experiencing this shift in care due to an arbitrary age. We had to do better.

In 2017, Gov. Branstad was appointed Ambassador to China by President Donald Trump. Thus, Lt. Gov. Kim Reynolds became Iowa's governor. I immediately briefed Gov. Reynolds about the situation. She readily embraced the need for change and due to her leadership, a willing legislature, an adaptive Department of Human Services, an excellent provider in *Child-Serve*, along with officials in the Trump administration, we finally got the provision we needed to serve young adults like Lucas with excellence. It just came 20 years after my initial presentation.

Thirty-one months after Lucas was inappropriately transitioned to a geriatric facility, he returned to *ChildServe* to a hero's welcome. Darla and I pondered then, as we do now, that this may have been God's purpose all along in allowing

Lucas to live as long as he did. Had Lucas passed away at age 10 or 14 or before his 22nd birthday, we may not have had the urgency to coordinate the needed levers for this change in policy and in service.

And because of Lucas' extended life, I believe God highlighted His mighty works through Gov. Reynolds, through legislators, through bureaucracy, through *ChildServe*, and through the federal administration.

Darla and I cheered and cried, as Lucas was admitted to a service provider that could meet his needs. My guess is so did Aaron's parents, along with other parents and families. Thanks to Lucas' life, many lives are being impacted through this honoring service change. And, hopefully and prayerfully, many more will be impacted for years to come. Praise God for using Lucas' life to display His mighty works!

As mentioned earlier, I don't believe God's mighty works were displayed through Lucas' disabilities, his limitations, nor his seizures. His mighty works are vibrantly displayed through our response to Lucas' imperfections. And for these acts of genuine love and action to meet Lucas' needs and the needs of Lucas' peers, we praise God.

There's no doubt Lucas' life changed my life, Darla's life, our family's life, and the lives of many others. I left my love for education. Darla forwent her career. Lucas' brothers didn't go to Disney World or national parks. They were constantly in the family Suburban visiting their brother.

Through all of this a special place called *Opportunities Unlimited* was given new life and new facilities and new programs to serve people with disabilities with excellence. Their mission of "maximizing personal potential through purposeful and dignified living" was and is lived out for many individuals and families. Praise God for His mighty works!

A camp for people with special needs was birthed at our family's kitchen table in Sioux City. Darla and I were thrilled to launch an organization in Sioux City to build a state-of-the-art camp for people with disabilities; a place where campers of all ages and abilities can participate in challenging activities and experience success.

Hiking, canoeing, and horseback riding should not be reserved for the "normal" – Camp High Hopes provides extraordinary opportunities for extraordinary boys and girls, men and women. This camp was given life through the inspiration of Lucas' life. Praise God for His mighty works!

An arbitrary system for serving young adults with medical complexities and special needs was changed. No longer is the bar of expectation for serving these unique young men and women limited to housing in a geriatric facility where grandpas and grandmas are fulfilling their last days. Instead, these unique needs are met with medical excellence while the culture and the outings inspire life and purpose. Praise God for His mighty works!

The ministry where Darla and I currently serve, *The FAMiLY Leader,* is passionate about ensuring all life, born and unborn, has opportunity to live out each planned and ordained day. Lucas' life inspires us to go to bat and to stand in the gap for life.

This is why we say, "Wow! Just flat out...wow!"

Lucas never said a word. He never took a step. He was incapable of voicing decisions on what to wear, where to go, what to eat, and who to see. Yet, as you can see, God's mighty works were displayed exponentially through Lucas's life.

And we believe Lucas' life will have generational impact through many ministries, through a multitude of policies and most definitely through our family. Yes, indeed, praise God for His mighty works!

But hold on, there's more. God's mightiest work was still to come...

God's mightiest work was reserved for Lucas at 4:40 a.m., Nov. 22, 2021. This is when Jesus transitioned Lucas to the best and most appropriate setting ever...Heaven. Not only did Lucas meet Jesus face-to-face, but every tear and every disability were wiped away. Talk about mighty works. Wow! Just flat out...wow!

As a friend reminded me, I don't believe it's any accident that Lucas passed away at 4:40 a.m.

When we read the Gospel of Luke, we read at chapter and verse 4:40, "All those who had anyone sick with various diseases (disabilities) brought them to Him (Jesus). As He (Jesus) laid His hands on each one of them, He would heal them."

Jesus is still in the healing, redemptive, and miracle business. And Darla and I believe Jesus healed Lucas and made him whole at 4:40 a.m.

All glory to God for His mighty works.
Afresh, we give thanks
for the gift and life of Lucas.
May his light shine on!

Epilogue

Darla and I just learned that Lucas' friend and housemate, Joey, passed away. Joey is the friend that knew Lucas' song. Joey was always a delight when Darla and I visited Lucas. So, immediately, upon learning the news we were choked up with sadness.

And, immediately, upon hearing the news we were glad for Joey's newfound freedom where he, too, received a new body and all his tears and disabilities were wiped away as he met Jesus face-to-face. Then, our spirits leapt with tears of joy as we imagined Joey and Lucas' heavenly reunion. Wow. Can you imagine what that had to be like? Talking, jumping, laughing, running, eating and then repeating. I wish I could have witnessed the look on each of their faces. One day we will. And, that day will be soon.

Darla and I didn't send out a friends and family Christmas card the short month after Lucas' funeral. Darla composed a New Year's greeting for 2022, however, she couldn't bring herself to send. So, let me conclude with the heart of Darla's message.

The phrase that seems to best describe our final year with Lucas is, "He gives and takes away. He gives and takes away." God gave many blessings...many beautiful days with a sweet granddaughter, many memorable times with family in Marco Island, in Columbus, in Jackson Hole and at our home in Iowa. In addition, He gave many opportunities with The

FAMiLY Leader to travel the country as we passionately pursue "A revived America that honors God and blesses people."

And then there was the huge gift on December 17 when God gave us a precious grandson, Dixon James. Dixon James' birth provided a much needed reminder that God is sovereign and He alone is the author and giver of life. To say Dixon's birth greatly assisted in our healing and coping with Lucas' death would be a vast understatement.

Our focus tangibly shifted from mourning the loss of Lucas' life to the celebration of Dixon's new life. We tangibly walked away from the shattered glass of a baby with issues to embracing Dixon's healthy new life with much thanksgiving.

Amid all these blessings, God took away our Lucas. While preparing for this possibility constantly over the course of Lucas' life, it still came as sudden...as a shock...as a why now. God took away our car rides, our songs, our readings, our naps, our kisses, our touch, our...Lucas. And to be transparent, there is no way to be prepared and ready for burying a child.

As God took away, He gave Lucas the best home ever, his eternal home. He gave Lucas a new body. He gave Lucas a heavenly home with streets of gold. He is giving Lucas strolls along the Sea of Chrystal. Yes, God gave and is giving much to Lucas.

The scriptures tells us frequently to "lift up our eyes." There's good reason for this encouragement. When we lift up our eyes, we see the big picture. And when we see the big picture, we rejoice for him and embrace that this life is but a mere breath. We'll be with Lucas soon. Thus, we are choosing to lift up our eyes and to sing with all of our hearts..."He gives and takes away. He gives and takes away. My heart will choose to say, Lord, blessed be your name."

Speaking of big picture, Dixon James' baptism was six months to the day of Lucas' passing. This baptism celebrated the new life of our grandson while recognizing God's greatest gift...the offer of eternal life. Dixon's birth and baptism are a great reminder "He gives and takes away. He gives..."

May you join us in choosing to sing with all of your hearts, "Lord, blessed be Your name."

Thank you for sharing this glimpse into our lives. I pray that the light from Lucas has blessed you and that you will find new inspiration to face your days with a little more faith, a little more hope, and a lot more love.

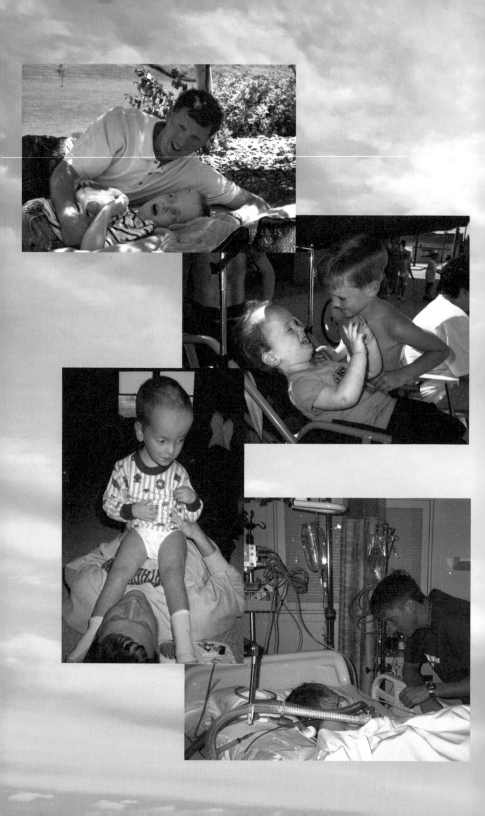

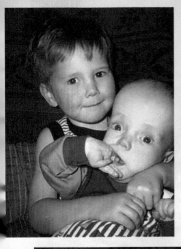

"We hope you are inspired by the light from Lucas as you let your light shine..."

MATTHEW 5:16

The Vander Plaats Family